DATE DUE

The Illusion of Prison Reform: Corrections in Canada

American University Studies

Series XI
Anthropology/Sociology

Vol. 5

PETER LANG
New York · Berne · Frankfurt am Main

Herbert Gamberg and
Anthony Thomson

The Illusion of Prison Reform

Corrections in Canada

PETER LANG
New York · Berne · Frankfurt am Main

Library of Congress Cataloging in Publication Data

Gamberg, Herbert.
 The illusion of prison reform.

 (American University Studies. Series XI, Anthropology/
sociology; vol. 5)
 Bibliography: p.
 1. Prisons – Canada. 2. Corrections – Canada.
3. Punishment – Canada. 4. Rehabilitation of criminals –
Canada. I. Thomson, Anthony, 1949–. II. Title.
III. Series.
HV9507.G36 1984   365'.973   83-49353
ISBN 0-8204-0093-9
ISSN 0740-0489

CIP-Kurztitelaufnahme der Deutschen Bibliothek

Gamberg, Herbert:
The illusion of prison reform: corrections
in Canada / Herbert Gamberg and Anthony
Thomson. – New York; Berne; Frankfurt am
Main: Lang, 1984.
 (American University Studies: Ser. 11,
 Anthropology, Sociology; Vol. 5)
 ISBN 0-8204-0093-9

NE: Thomson, Anthony; American University
Studies / 11

© Peter Lang Publishing, Inc., New York 1984

Printed by Lang Druck, Inc., Liebefeld/Berne (Switzerland)

TABLE OF CONTENTS

CHAPTER ONE

INTRODUCTION

This study is about prisons in Canada, the body of ideas which justify them, and the meaning of attempts to change them. The prison, which processes those whom other institutions define as problems, is itself a social problem, a living embodiment of social failure. It is rare in modern societies to find those who do not consider the locking of human beings in cages as being a somewhat shameful event. At best, such treatment is considered a necessary evil.

Like most relatively durable social institutions, the prison is imbedded in a wider social and historical context. Its existence and operation cannot be explained without reference to its history in the total society. The existence of prisons has been defended by a common ideological tradition within which there have been periodic criticisms, controversy and attendant reform. The demand for prison reform has been an endemic feature of Canadian and North American prison history. At the same time, the more conservative-minded have demanded a return to first principles, that prisons are no place to mollycoddle criminals who need a stern dose of discipline and control. It is our contention that the swings between reform of a specific type and "law and order", swings which proponents on both sides see as diametrically opposed positions, are really only swings within one common body of ideological assumptions. We hope to break out of this ideological mold and to critically evaluate whether the common assumptions about prisons and the programmes that derive from them may be part of a social problem rather than a resolution of social problems.

In the face of the reality of a prison, a collection of people caged in an immense mass of concrete and steel, the most fundamental questions about the nature of crime appear in sharp relief. The prison exists because crime exists. Questions about the very status of crime as a concept--how social transgressions should be defined and by whom--have led to a wide variety of thoughts about the problem, even recently to a school of criticism which would choose to "de-prison" society. An analysis of attempts to change the prison must come to grips with the attempts to deal with crime, with old-style justifications and well as social reformers and modern critical theory.

To put into prison, or to incarcerate, people because they have committed certain misdeeds of a socially defined and changing nature has not been universal in all societies. It is obvious that societies which depended for their livelihood on hunting animals and gathering edible plants, and were therefore always on the move, could not carry lock-ups around with them

for whatever miscrerants did arise. Rather these simpler
societies commonly handled the breaking of social rules by
other means than prison and, in those cases where sterner
measures were required, actual banishment from the society
often served somewhat the same purpose as contemporary imprisonment. Whether such societies actually produced less
behaviour which warranted harsh measures and whether more
complicated advanced societies are more conducive to criminal
behaviour has been a subject of much debate in social thought.
Regardless of one's answer to the question of the greater
harmony of tribal societies, the fact is that they were without
prisons and that prisons as we know them are a relatively
recent historical phenomenon. Of course, there have been advanced societies without prisons, for if all prisoners were
killed, transported or consigned to the galleys, as Kirkpatrick
asserts (1965), "there would be no need for a correctional
system." In the last three centuries, however, a more humane
approach to the problem has ruled out such a drastic response
to crime, and the prison has become the central feature of
modern penology, ideologically if not in terms of the number of
individuals processed.

Prisons are only one part of a larger phenomenon called
corrections. Corrections is that broad field of ideas, programmes and institutions which have developed over time to
attempt to change the behaviour of specific types of offenders, to mend their ways and transform them into "law-abiding
citizens". The prison is only one instrument in the social
array of institutions which have developed in part to change
the conduct of a person convicted of a crime. The term "person
convicted of a crime" is used rather than "criminal" because
the latter term connotes some vast abyss between those in
prison and the model citizens in the rest of society, an
assumption which we believe to be implicit in most correctional
programmes.

The field of corrections as an approach to the "crime
problem" has intrinsic limitations. In the first place, these
limitations derive from the fact that correctional programmes
deal only with people after they have been convicted of a
crime. This means that all those people who commit crimes and
are never caught are not acted upon by any correctional programme. Moreover, the question of the nature of the crime, the
social factors which cause crime, and the social changes which
may be necessary to create an harmonious society are outside
the purview of corrections as commonly conceived. To attempt
to alter someone's behaviour after he has been caught does
not, by definition, have much to do with the creation of a
crime-free society, that is, with real crime prevention.

This is an important point since those who are engaged in
treating the convicted criminal population, whether this treatment emphasizes reformation and rehabilitation or punishment,

often see their jobs as effecting the rate of crime in general.
If corrections were working their best, they would turn all
convicted persons (a small proportion of actual law breakers)
into law-abiding citizens, (which, it has been amply demonstrated, it does not do). In studying the history, social
roots and ideological validations of corrections, we are, in a
way, explaining how and why this field has developed and continues to foster a false image of itself. In this way, while
not presenting a full theory of crime and its prevention, we
hope to explicate the ideological implications of many theories
which suffuse the correctional endeavour.

The empirical focus of this monograph is the changing
ideological context of prison policies which have overlain a
relatively recent reformative trend with a revived emphasis on
segregation and punishment. We discuss a variety of recent
programmes and techniques which have been devised to attempt to
deter people from recommitting acts or to punish them in specific doses of severity. While many programmes have developed
outside of prisons, especially those in the most recent wave of
reform, imprisonment remains the treatment of last resort in
corrections. The primary question is to account for the
failure of this latest reform ripple. This will inevitably
lead us into some consideration of the general problem of state
finances in a period of contemporary economic recession. But
ideological change in general cannot be reduced to simple
economic reflexes. This is perhaps more apparent in the case
of the prison than any other social institution. It has been
demonstrated that alternatives to imprisonment are less costly
in straight financial terms than continuing to maintain large
populations in prison fortresses, yet the recent return to so-
called first principles of punishment and the greater use of
imprisonment, is associated with government restraint in other
areas. The logical response that with increased social dis-
tresss there is a need for the state to expand the institutions
of repression is too simple. Rather, the prison is also fundamentally a symbol; it fulfills a necessary ideological function
in the canons of social control.

The prison has specific defining characteristics which
give it an enduring appeal as a place to manage people defined
as criminals. It is a definite physical array of buildings
which segregate and restrict the usual freedom of a convicted
population. Since society at large can be presented with the
image that a good part of its criminals are tucked away where
they cannot continue the acts considered dangerous or reprehen-
sible, so the illusion is bred that prisons separate the
healthy societal body from its unhealthy parts. And insofar as
the prison population cannot usually, while in prison,
adversely affect the rest of the population, the inmate's lack
of freedom frees the rest of society from their potential
crimes. Along with an older appeal to vengence, it is this
supposedly sanitizing function which has made the prison the

centre of the correction process.

The prison is different, however, from other total institutions or institutions which have the right to control all
the behaviour of its client population, such as mental institutions. This difference is built not only into the greater
array of punishments exercised by a prison, but results from
the different nature of the inmates of prisons. The person
convicted of a crime and sent to prison is always considered,
at some level, responsible for the acts which sent him there.
There would be great range of debate about how responsible a
convicted criminal is for his crime from those who consider him
the total individual cause of his misdeed to those who see him
totally forced by social circumstances into acts whose criminal
character is even quetioned. Even in the latter case, the most
radical interpretation still considers an inmate responsible
enough to comprehend why other factors than himself are to
blame for his imprisonment. While such responsibility may be
surmised for some parts of the patient population in a mental
hospital, it would still be admitted that a truly mentally ill
person can bear no responsibility for his acts. The same line
of argument would hold for schoolchildren especially at the
younger ages. The prison inmate is supposed to be a normal
physically and mentally functioning adult member of society who
has committed some act in respect of which he has been caught
and which legally defines imprisonment as the cost he must
bear.

Prison in also a punitive institution. This seems obvious,
but it is not always so to some reformers or to some people who
believe that higher spiritual suffering is the only kind worth
talking about ("Stone walls do not a prison make"). The former
would basically like to humanize the institution while leaving
its confining and segregating char-acteristics intact. Many of
the prison reforms initiated over the years, which not only
attempt to better the physical conditions of prisons but move
towards collective forms of decision making by inmates themselves begin with the assumption that prison can be made into
relatively pleasant places to live. We shall discuss some of
these reforms, many of which we consider necessary and good
changes to an essentially repressive institution, but we think
it an illusion to consider that these changes transform prison
into something else. As long as adults are locked up with no
choice to leave of their own free will and they are not treated
as mentally or physically ill, then they are in prison and that
confinement is unpleasant to them. It is extremely rare for a
prison inmate not to wish to leave the prison regardless of the
level of amenities provided there. Those rare cases of prisoners being confined for so long that they are uncomfortable in
society indicate that dependence can become psychologically
debilitating. People might of course choose to remain in a
place which provided many conveniences and pleasures with no
obligations, but this would be less a prison and more a resort.

Thus although the purely retributive aspect of prisons has diminished as a principle over the years, prison still remains a place which is inherently punishing (Davies 1974; Cohen and Taylor 1972).

It is even more punishing in the average prison in Canada where the reform ideal is little more than an ideal and where confinement and repressive control remain the order of the day. Brutality, indignity and anonymity, the deprivation of taken for granted rights in a relentless succession of minutes turning into hours, into days, months and years is the core of the prison experience, an experience which the inmate very aptly calls "doing time." Even today Canadian prisons still employ solitary confinement as a normal instrument of punishment. Michael Enright sums the Canadian prison experience well when he says (1977) that "inmates in almost every institution complain of brutal treatment at the hands of their keepers and cry out for simple gestures of dignity." While reformers decry the failure of rehabilitation, the "practice of caging a man to make him repent has become a celebration of despair behind the stone-grey wall."

Unless one accepts the usual but bizaare interpretation that rebellion by prison inmates is not due to their conditions but to their inherently criminogenic nature, then the periodic and common prison rebellions which mark the history of Canadian prisons attest to their oppressive atmosphere. These rebellions, significantly called "riots" by the prison administration and the media, are the events which set in motion the ideolgical clash between those who think that rebellion is proof that prison is too harsh and those who think that rebellion is a symptom that prison is too soft. Regardless of the debate, however, the negative response to miserable prison conditions continues unabated. On the National Prison Justice Day in 1978, the Canadian penitentiary service indicated that about 3500 of the 9300 men in federal prison participated in a peaceful strike by refusing to eat or work. The leaders of the protest announced to the media that twenty-six men and women had died of unnatural causes in federal prisons that year-- eleven of them suicides and eight murdered. The report also stressed that in many cases death was a result of prisoners being put into solitary confinement. Even under usual circumstances, imprisonment is inherently punishing. In the words of the American Friends Service Committee, imprisonment "denies autonomy, degrades dignity, impairs or destroys self-reliance, inculcates authoritarian values...,fractures family ties...and prejudices the prisoner's future prospects" (1971).

Prisons are violent places. During the first three months of 1983 there were 51 incidents of self-mutilation in Canadian federal prisons (Ross 1983: 17). Suicides also increased dramatically in 1983. During the two previous years, for example, two prisoners had committed suicide in Atlantic Canadian prisons. In 1983 this figure jumped to eight, including the first ever in the provincial minimum security prison. This increase led to the formation of a Committee of Inquiry to attempt to explain the reason for the sudden jump in suicides and to recommend appropriate changes.

The maintenance of a prison system is costly not only in the human price paid both by those who are incarcerated and those whose livelihood is derived from the onerous task of standing guard on the prison population, but it is costly in straight financial terms. In 1966 the correctional system in Canada cost $0.6 billion. Over the next ten years this figure more than doubled (Jobson 1977:254). By 1983 the federal prison system cost $1.5 billion. This money houses the 11,300 prisoners confined in federal penitentiaries, an increase of about 2000 since 1977. According to the Parliamentary Sub-Committee on the Penitentiary System (1977), it cost $17,515 annually for each male prisoner. Given that the proportion of offenders serving time who have been reconvicted of crimes is up to 75%, even short term inmates spend long periods in prison at these tremendous costs. Twenty-five years of prison is a financial burden of $400,000, and this amount of imprisonment is not unusual (:35). The less expensive parole system, which complements the prison, spends $1400 per offender, so the burden continues after release (:35-36). Fewer than 30% of applications from those who are eligible for parole are granted by the National Parole Board (Hackler and Gould 1981: 408; Waller,1971), a proportion which is half that of the previous decade (Cousineau and Veevers 1972: 144).

The human and financial costs of the prison system are only a symptom of the problem of Canadian corrections. Prison is not the place that really treats the problem of crime in Canadian society. There are always differences between crimes reported and offenders convicted and sentenced. Hidden behind this difference is the whole social bias of the police appre-hension and sentencing processes. 68% of all male admissions in 1975 were 18-29 years old; 81% had not had more than grade 10 schooling, while only 3% had any education beyond high school. The prison population is therefore heavily weighted toward young males of low social and economic status (Phillips and Votey 1972). The reason for their conviction involves acts of illegally acquiring money or goods which comprise about 70% of admissions (see Fitzgerald and Sims 1979). The propor-tion of prisoners in prison who had been sentenced for violent offenses was 62% in 1980 (Hackler and Gould 1981: 409). Almost half of these were sentenced for robbery. The proportion of violent offenders in the prison system has grown steadily since the middle 1970s. The lengthening of sentences which accompa-nied the 1976 restriction of the death penalty ensures that prisoners convicted of violent crimes will remain in the prison longer. They now often comprise the majority of those incar-cerated at a given time, a condition which makes for a mass of

desperate and alienated inmates. The tendency to hand down
longer sentences in the early 1980s also caused a jump in the
prison population. Canada already has a reputation for being
especially punitive (Tepperman 1977) and for having one of the
highest rates of imprisonment in the western world (Hogarth
1967). This is despite the finding that increased incarceration only has a mininal effect on crime prevention (Greenberg
1976). While longer-term sentences for violent crimes are
creating a log-jam in the prison, the usual length of sentence
along with the type of crime committed indicates that the great
majority of Canadians who have been imprisoned have not been
significantly dangerous to life and limb. 65% of Canadian male
prisoners are sentenced to less than five years (Jobson
1977:254; Statistics Canada 1975: 23-5). The types of crimes
concomitant with the rate of recidivism demonstrate that a very
small number of people who commit small property offenses get
incarcerated once, twice and many times (Giffin 1966); these
unfortunate few make up the bulk of the long-term Canadian
prison population.

The overall failure of the correctional system to affect
the convicted offender has led to periodic attempts to reform
the correctional system, to change the prison toward a more
rehabilitative rather than punitive institution, and to ini-
tiate a variety of procedures to rehabilitate offenders in less
expensive social contexts outside the prison. While these
reforms may be supported to the extent that they reduce the
population in prison, none of them gets to the nub of the
problem facing Canadian corrections.

A common body of assumptions and theories about crime and
punishment has undergirded the history of treatment of convicted offenders in Canada. Exposure of this ideological
understructure, the reforms that have been devised to supposedly change it while remaining trapped in its vise, and the
social consequences of the continuation of this ideological
structure is the subject of this book. The main focus is a
review of the development of the post-1945 version of the
rehabilitative ethic and an analysis of the programmes which
were established within the parameters of this philosophy.

Two points need to be addressed with respect to this
monograph, both of a contextual nature. Although Canadian
experience has its own specificity, correctional ideologies in
Canada are connected in a number of ways with developments
elsewhere, particularly in Britain and the United States, and
therefore are part of a wider Western context. Chapters Two,
Three and Four deal with the broad social and historical background which has defined the correctional field in Europe and
the United States to the present time, and the principal philosophical positions with respect to law and order and reformation. Chapter Five provides an overview of the "new deal" in
penitentiaries in the post-1945 period. The 1960s witnessed

both a critical response in criminological circles to all that
had gone before in corrections and a new ripple of attempted
reform measures. The period was one of extreme significance in
dramatizing the way in which a high degree of critical response
to the prison experience becomes institutionalized in an endem-
ically conservative system. In this sense, the recent history
of reforms may represent a rather typical mode by which the
correctional system reacts to a concerted attack upon its
taken-for-granted premises. While the reform measures have
proved to be old wine in new bottles, these phenomena are
symptomatic of the real crisis in Canadian and Western
corrections. Chapter Seven will evaluate critically some
aspects of a "new criminology" which has responded to this
latest crisis.

If this study is bounded by time, with a concentration on
the developments of the prison system in the so-called welfare
state, it is also bounded spatially. Canadian experience is
also specific because, although ideologies and programmes have
a "national" origin usually in Central Canada, their
implementation will vary according to regional histories and
conditions. The empirical observations recounted in this
monograph have been derived from a study of the federal
penitentiary system in Atlantic Canada. Chapter Six provides a
descriptive analysis of the therapeutic community, one of the
show-piece reforms of the medical model in corrections.
Chapter Eight reviews the rise and modifications of the trend
towards community-oriented corrections. Following this,
Chapter Nine argues that, with official recognition of the
failure of prisoner rehabilitation, the most recent trend in
corrections is towards a more punitive model. A conclusion
will sum up our general finding about corrections and the place
of reform within it while pointing, if only skeletally, toward
a rethinking of the endeavour.

CHAPTER TWO

RETRIBUTION AND REFORMATION

Introduction

The question of how best to protect society from those
people within it who are defined as criminals has been a continuing problem in the history of complex societies. While the
system of punishment used in the West stems from a combination
of philosophical traditions and material needs arising in con-
junction with the development of capitalism, certain crucial
conceptions have much deeper roots.

Prior to the development of a central governing authority,
acts which violated group norms were dealt with locally by the
People concerned. Offenders were treated according to the
principle of individual retaliation, largely a question of
revenge and retribution (Martzen 1974). The target of the
sanction was the individual or his family. As political power
became further centralized, social control bacame increasingly
the prerogative of the state and punishment was administered by
the decree of the sovereign. Penal sanctions were brutal,
arbitrary and public (Sellin 1972; Foucault 1978).

While the agency for administering the punishment was
transferred from the individual to the state, the development
of imprisonment as a common sanction was grafted onto earlier
conceptions. Prior to the eighteenth century, religious doc-
trines held undisputed ideological sway in Western Europe. The
general religious orientation to the question of crime and
punishment rested on a view of the other-worldly meaning of
both goodness and evil. The rationale of punishment rested on
a religious ideology which essentially considered the human
soul to be a battleground between the forces of darkness and
light which operated through the agency of the individual human
being. The most extreme versions of this ideology rested on
notions of predestination, the belief that the other-worldly
disposition of the soul was decided before birth. Some were
the elect and could expect rewards in the after-life; others
were damned and no amount of good works could theoretically
pull them through. This conception was based on an absolute
separation between good and evil, a metaphysical notion which
has continually reappeared in different, more sophisticated,
ideological orientations towards the question of criminality.

There was a contradiction inherent in this absolute hiatus
between the elect and the non-elect, and the administration of
punishment, because of the question of individual responsibility. If the human body was the unwilling vessel of evil
intent, the responsibility for the criminal act did not rest

individual, but rather with original sin. However, the commission of an evil act was not usually seen merely as a passive happenstance over which the individual had no control, but rather as the result of succumbing to temptation, there being hypothetically the power to resist and remain in the state of grace. Ideologically, the basis of punishment rested on a religious model which postulated a dichotomy between good and evil people, and justified punishment as an attempt to restore the individual to a state of grace through the infliction of suffering. Structurally, the state acted both to consolidate the traditions of common law and popular justice under its authority, and to protect privileged social groups from the depredations of those with opposed interests.

Within this retributive response to acts deemed criminal there were correctional motives as well as implicit notions of both general and particular deterrence. Besides exacting retribution for an act defined as criminal, it was expected that the punishment would directly deter the particular offender from continuing to act in a criminal way through fear of further punishment. General deterrencew refers to the effect that punishing an offender is expected to have on others who are made to fear a similar fate should they break the law. One primary motive for remaining within the law, then, is thought to be the desire to avoid punishment. The amputation of a hand as punishment for stealing has a certain barbaric logic in relation to the particular case and the infliction of corporal or capital punishment in public view was meant to serve as more than mere entertainment for a population we assume to be more callous and brutal than our own. It was a warning to deter the potential criminal from transgressing the authority of the sovereign.

This justification of punishment included a notion of individual reformation in the general sense that actions short of capital punishment which culminate in the return of the transgressor to the population are based on the supposition that people can change, in this case, that people can learn to resist temptation. While evilness can never be overcome in this world, it was still considered possible to change some individuals, although certain people could never be redeemed--they incarnated evil and could not be saved.

Classical Criminology

During the eighteenth century a revolutionary break with the past occurred in all fields. Based on a fundamental change in the organization of society, alternative conceptions of social organization were devised. The institutions and ideas which survived from the pre-modern era were subject to withering criticism. The right of the King to impose arbitrary punishments was rejected, along with a whole host of other ideas associated with divine right monarchy. In this period of

Enlightenment, the legitimacy of an appeal to the supernatural was undercut. Evil was stripped of its other-worldly meaning and the imposition of the most cruel and degrading punishments, as revenge or retribution for acts defined as criminal, was attacked (Tappan, 1960:585).

In place of the feudal conception of a supernaturally ordained order, the enlightenment thinkers theorized that nature operated according to its own inherent laws which were discoverable by reason. Similarly, in the realm of human conduct, there were discoverable natural laws. Society was composed of individuals, unique egos, endowed with natural inalienable rights. Each man pursued his own self-interest and, through competition, the best individuals would rise to the top and each would receive the reward which they had earned.

This process of pursuing individual advantage, however, contained within it the threat of infringing upon the rights of others. The state (meaning the apparatuses of government as well as controlling organs such as the armed forces and the judiciary) was charged with the task of defending individuals from these infringements. Legal statues were to be consistent with natural law and the laws of "eternal reason". The criminal was deemed responsible for his actions; consequently, the possibility existed that the criminal could come to understand through his own reason that he had contravened natural law. Having chosen to infringe the natural rights of fellow citizens, criminals became outlaws and forfeited, at least for a time, many of their own rights (Vogelman 1968:360). The offender received both moral condemnation and punishment (Jones 1965) at the hands of the designated agents of the state.

The classical school of criminology developed during this period as a reaction to the capriciousness of feudal justice. The most outstanding early figure in the field of penology was Cesare Bonesara, Marchese di Beccaria, an Italian jurist. His On Crimes and Punishment attacked the use of torture and mutilation, and advanced the view that punishment was justified only on the grounds of deterrence: fear would prevent both the actual and the potential criminal from breaking the law. The ends of deterrence were better met by the certainty of punishment rather than its severity. Such views were associated with reforms in the administration of criminal justice (Radzinowicz 1966; Vold 1958).

In England the utilitarian, Jeremy Bentham, applied the principle that people were motivated positively by pleasure and negatively by pain as a rationale for the punishment of offenders. The potential criminal would be deterred from crime when the pleasure anticipated from the crime was less than the amount of suffering which would result from being caught (Barnes and Teeters 1951). The continuing dominance of the prevailing conceptions of retribution, retaliation and revenge, however, required that the total emphasis remained on the application of the principle of pain. Since the individual had rationally chosen to act in an unlawful way, deterrence by punishment seemed the only logical and satisfying response.

This emphasis on certain and definite punishment with rationally determined sentences of escalating severity was modified, both in theory and practice, in two directions. Children and lunatics were not deemed to possess the necessary faculty of reason; consequently, they were not fully responsible for their actions. Since they were thereby delegitimated as responsible agents, the full provisions of the law had to be suspended. Secondly, the realization that abstract "equal" standards did not apply equally in concrete cases led to the practice of recognizing judicial discretion in sentencing. These modifications formed aspects of what became known as "neo-classicism" in criminal law (Cressey 1972).

Classicism was clearly an advance over the previously prevailing religious views. While the dichotomy between good and evil people remained, this conception was modified by postulating degrees of evilness. Although the debunking of the mediating supernatural elements of religious mythology was progressive, the new philosophy shared similar assumptions of philosophical idealism: its other-wordly foundation was re-placed by "eternal reason". The recognition that the social structure was more than the rational balance of individual wills awaited the development of modern mass production and the advancement of natural science. Both metaphysical and classi-cal conceptions continue to influence the administration of criminal law (Jones 1965:` 3). The religious conception, which emphasized moral culpability, was compatible with the classical notion of the freedom of will. In the religious conception of crime, less importance had been placed on reason. The criminal was not expected to understand fully what he had done wrong; he had rather to recognize, in a purely instrumental way, that his actions had contradicted divine scripture. Classicism con-tained logically the purely intellectual possibility of deducing by logic the "natural laws" which had been contra-vened, and criminals, similarly, could come to comprehend these "natural" rules. This blending of reason and religion formed the core of the ideology of penitence and the penitentiary.

Classical thinkers had advocated the determination of explicit legal formulations stipulating a hierarchy of penal-ties for progressively severe infractions of the natural moral code. Punishment was logically to be measured in an amount greater than the criminal gain (Radzinowicz 1966: 11-12), and be dispensed in known and rationally determined quantifiable doses. The use of imprisonment as a form of punishment was logically consistent with the classical approach which con-sidered the loss of liberty to be sufficient punishment and easily apportioned in quantifiably greater amounts for progressively heinous crimes.

The Rise of the Penitentiary

The banishment of criminals is a logical corollary of the absolute separation of good and evil. The purification of the society by the removal of those parts considered to be unwholesome has an ancient history. By the sixteenth century, one common form of banishment used in Britain was transportation: criminals were removed from the community and sent to the American colonies usually as indentured servants. After the Revolution of 1776, and before the resumption of transportation to Australia (Barnes 1972: 114) the convicted population remained confined in England in prison hulks. Hulks were large vessels which, being no longer sea-worthy, were tied up permanently in ports. The prisoners were not differentiated, and some chidren and obvious lunatics were confined in the hulk together with the rest. The resumption of transportation to the new Pacific colonies lasted until the early part of the nineteenth century when the problem of banishment had to be solely confronted within the confines of the nation state.

The idea of imprisonment grew out of the accumulated experience of several centuries use of workhouses, houses of corrections and jails normally used to house debtors (Pugh 1968). The institutions already at hand were converted into the early prisons. In England they combined elements of puritan ethics which were compatible with the early development of wage-labour. Like the Houses of Correction, they were designed with the intention of teaching the poor habits of industriousness and thrift. The heritage of social control of these disciplinary institutions was grafted onto the new prison system when this was established. The roots of the prison, then, extend back to straight confinement with an additional imperative of moral training. In the early eighteenth century a British jail was a business enterprise. The prisoner could be charged a fee for admission, for a bed and even for the irons he wore: the more irons the higher the charges. The privilege of being a warden or keeper, with rights to the profits made from the prisoners, could be bought and sold (Walker 1972: 83-84). If the prisoner were poor, which was often the case since the most common cause of imprisonment was defaulting on a debt, then during the time he was confined his bill would increase while his chances for release would decrease. With the exception of these unfortunates, the most common type of people confined for substantial periods would be those awaiting trail and those incarcerated for religious or political offences (Barnes 1972: 114).

During the late eighteeneth century, especially after 1776 in the United States and 1789 in France, imprisonment became the usual means to punish offenders. This practice was consistent with the classical philosophy of a carefully measured scale of punishment based on a uniform standard of suffering: length of confinement. The dreadful condition of the early jails, associated with their haphazard development, were gradually exposed by the efforts of such reformers as John Howard in England. While he was opposed to the wretched conditions of the jails, and the corrupt and inefficient practices of the local justices, which he exposed in The State of Prisons in England and Wales, Howard was an advocate of efficient administration as well as individual reformation through solitude and hard work (King and Morgan 1980: 1). The prison was supposed to combine deterrence, reform and punishment with humanitarianism (Ignatieff 1981: 160).

While physical conditions in these early jails were deplorable, historians claim that they had a considerably complex internal social order and that the control of the keepers was tenuous. Prisoners had considerable autonomy and the 18th century inmate community, which had sometimes a "family" atmosphere (Ignatieff, 1981:161), exercised a considerable degree of independent control (1978:38). This was replaced with a new prison system, with its strict authoritarian measures and rules of silence and lock-step which were designed to break up this collectivity, to stamp out the community and sub-culture of the confined and assert the power of the prison administration and the guards (1981: 161). Prisoners were to be segregated and held under a strict discipline by a hierarchical system of authority (Fitzgerald and Sim 1979: 142; Matheson 1974). This new regime of discipline, surveillance and control was common to prisons, asylums, workhouses, juvenile reformatories and industrial schools. They all evinced "a common belief in the reformative powers of enforced asceticism, hard labour, religious instruction and solitude" (Ignatieff, 1981:162.

Consequently in several countries, new institutions of punishment were constructed or converted,grey stone fortresses which looked like misplaced relics from the Middle Ages, and were designed to strike terror into the criminal and control the population through fear: "The exterior of the prison", according to an 1848 encyclopedia, "should...be formed in the heavy and sombre style which most frequently impresses the spectator with gloom and terror" (quoted in Johnston 1973: 26-27). "Ideal" prisons were devised, such as Bentham's Panopticon, architecturally conceived around one central surveillance point from which the various wings housing the prisoners could be constantly watched.

The develpment of an institution specializing in the confinement and surveillance of the "criminal population" was one part of the expansion of a centralized state authority. The prison was one of several institutions, including the asylum, the training school and the work house, which were created in response to the problems of social control created by the development of industrial capitalism (Rothman 1971). The prison was designed to reform and discipline the deviant and to routinize the habits of the poor (Foucault 1978). It was "part of a broader history of the struggle to establish a capitalist social order". Designed to control the "marginal elements of the working class", the prison came to have a lasting symbolic and ideological significance (Fitzgerald and Sim 1979: 140-141). Prisons removed from the labour market the least economically active members (Braverman 1974). In addition to the problems caused by the decline of transportation, and the philosophical under-pinning provided by classical theory, the rise of the prison was also connected with the desire to confine a body of potential workers in order to exploit their labour. This orientation was particularly common in North America (Sellin 1972).

American Institutional Development

While the prison has European theoretical origins, much of its early institutional development took place in the United States, which became the principal source for Canadian inspiration. The first experiments of note were undertaken in Philadelphia following the intervention of the Philadelphia Society for Alleviateing the Misery of Public Prisons (Tappan 1960: 605). The Society advocated reforming the practice of imprisonment through the development of a regime of solitary confinement coupled with hard labour, measures which were presented as reforms in two senses. First, the brutal treatment of prisoners, including such practices as corporal punisment, was to be eliminated as a form of retaliation for crimes. This was consistent with a classical perspective which would substitute imprisonment for physical brutality. Second, the changes proposed in the prison regime were thought to be reformative of the prisoners themselves. "Reforms", then, are generally of two types: those concerned with the practice of imprisonment affecting the conditions of oppression, and those concerned with the "reformation" of the character or personality of prisoner.

The programme of the Philadelphia Society was partially implemented as public policy in the construction of the Eastern and Western Penitentiaries, which embodied the Pennsylvania System. Corporal punishment was retained as a means of punishment for "crimes" committed against the prison regime, which was very harsh (Osborne 1916: 93-110). Consistent with the Quaker origin of imprisonment in North America, the Pennsylvania System had a strong religious orentation. Prisoners were confined to solitary single cells and forbidden to talk to one another--a restriction which was enforced by corporal punishment. The reform which elminated the physical infliction of pain as a punishment for criminal acts was undermined when corporal punishments such as whipping were reintroduced into the prison in order to maintain social control. In the solitude of their cells, prisoners were expected to reflect on their crime and become penitent, hence the term "penitentiary". It was assumed that the prison sentence would permit the prisoners an opportunity to take the time to reform themselves by coming to accept that they had sinned and then consciously adopting Christian morality (Neier 1976: 134). Consequently they were permitted to read from the Bible--the only reform facility provided--and the prison chaplain became the principal ideologue of the penitentiary system.

It was not only a matter of emphasis that the punitive aspects of this system far outweighed a rudimentary conception of religiously-inspired personal salvation; punishment itself was to be the catalytic agent which would convince a reasonable person to reform. This conception of personal change was thoroughly spiritualist in nature--by individual contemplation the prisoner was expected to be overwhelmed by his sense of guilt and then consciously choose the path of moral responsibility. The "silent system" was to provide the conditions for this individual reformation, and the provision of a Bible reflected an age in which there was litle uncertainty over the correctness of the prevailing ideology and the necessity, for reformation, of imbibing a determined world view. It is clear that the development of the classical school, despite an emphasis on reason, did not totally supersede the metaphysical view but, on the contrary, incorporated many aspects as integral parts of the new penal philosophy. Prisons, at least in their ideology, became in part the instruments which were to facilitate the religious conversion.

The supernatural attributes of temptation were partially undermined by rationalism, but the conception of an individual flaw was retained. The criminal was not only evil but also morally weak, having succumbed to temptations which the morally upright could resist. Imprisonment served the purpose of removing the offender from the social environment within which he had yielded to criminal behaviour and placing him in a sanitized environment (Neier 1976) in which he could repent and gain moral strength. Consequently prisons were built in rural areas away from cities, making communication with both relatives and friends difficult. Both of these provisions were intended to sever any connections between the individual and supposed negative influence in his environment (Sellin 1972) while emphasizing social repugnance.

Consistent with its origin, which emphasized the spiritual benefits to be derived from the regimen of work, the prisoners in the Pennsylvania System were expected to labour in individual handicraft work in their solitary cells. The use of solitary confinement in Pennsylvania had the predictable effect of driving many prisoners to suicide or insanity. In addition, the individual workshop idea was obsolescent. It reflected a past tradition of handicraft production which was slowly being replaced by mass production methods (Murton 1976: 11). The Pennsylvania model was gradually abandoned in the United States, although it had a greater influence on European prisons (:25), and was replaced by the Auburn system which had been implemented first in New York.

Like the Pennsylvania system, Auburn did not rely on individual penitence alone but rather placed its attempt at positive transformation on more practical grounds, while meeting the imperatives of the economy, by introducing labour into the prisons (Barnes 1972: 142-143). Unlike the solitary labour of Pennsylvania, however, the convicts worked together in congregate cells, and only at night were they kept in solitary confinement.

Given the social control origins of the prison, the debate between these alternative systems was couched in terms of individual reformation. It was claimed that the Pennsylvania model made the deepest impression on the souls of the prisoners and could potentially make more honest citizens; it could induce a qualitative change in a few. The Auburn system could produce a greater number of obedient citizens but had less effect on the prisoners' character beyond this overt compliance (Allen and Simorsen 1975).

Reformation was by no means the primary motive for introducing collective work: the origin of the prison system was connected to the desire to confine manpower and make it exploitable. Prisons were expected to become financially profitable, and a whole host of lease and labour programmes were operated in U.S. prisons up until the Second World War. One early state prison in the United States, for example, was located in a mine (Sellin 1972: 11-12). Hard labour was introduced for the purposes of punishment and profit. Ideological justifications dove-tailed with these practical considerations.

Canada's first penitentiary opened at Kingston in 1835 folowing the model of artisanal labor. Artisans in the town feared the competition of prison handicrafts work in such areas as shoe-making and advocated road work and the use of treadmills as suitable alternatives (Palmer 1980). At the time of Confederation in 1867, two further prisons had been built: St. Jean and "Rockhead" prisons in the East (Topping 1930: 68; Kidman 1947). The British North America Act gave legislative jurisdiction over penitentiaries to the Federal government and jurisdiction over reformatories and jails to the provinces. It made no provision for the terms of imprisonment and an arbitrary division according to the length of sentence grew up after 1867 to allocate prisoners to the different institutions. Offenders sentenced to two or more years confinement were sent to federal prisones while those serving under two years were imprisoned in provincial facilities (Fortanaro 1965: 302). Late in the 19th century the penal system in Canada underwent a major expansion.

The Positive Tradition

The nineteenth century witnessed the enormous expansion of technology which resulted from the application of social scientific knowledge to capitalist production. This tremendous success of the natural sciences put into relief the poverty of the knowledge of human behaviour. The first reaction of this situation was the attempt to derive laws of social behaviour which would be analogous to the laws thought to govern physics or chemistry, an attempt associated with the development of Positive Philosophy.

Positivism in criminology, from the Italian Lombroso onwards, utilized a model derived from the natural sciences in order to undertake the objective study of criminality, abandoning any concern with moral character and explicitly denying free will in the process (Wolfgang 1960). Two strands in the "deterministic" approach to criminality have been identified-- those which are biological in origin and attribute criminal action to inherited constitutional factors, and those which postulate environmental causation (Radzinowicz 1966). While these opposing views have contradictory implications for reform, they both reject the classical assumption of rational will. Since criminality is defined as largely outside the control of the individual, the justification of punishment on the grounds of moral culpability is undermined.

Criminologists subsequently rejected the various crude physical notions which derived from a too literal application of the natural science model to human affairs represented, for example, by Social Darwinism (Hofstadter 1955). The belief that criminality was inherited in the same fashion as blue eyes represented the continuation of the metaphysical notion, here in more "scientific" guise, that criminals were somehow very different from the majority of society.

Without necessarily rejecting the possibility of congenitally influenced behaviour, social scientists in the west subsequently emphasized the complex interplay between the social structure and the character development of the individual. As social determination undercut the justification of retributive punishment in the classical model, the positivists were faced with the contradiction of reconciling social causation with individual responsibility.

To solve this dilemma the positivists had recourse to the notion that "society" was an ultimate good and hence to breach its laws was a moral offense. (Jones 1965: 7). Criminals did not transgress the natural order so much as the social order. The argument that the compulsion to obey social laws was dependent upon the correspondence of these laws with the natural

rights of man was replaced by the view of the state as a
neutral institution which was above society and reconciled the
best interests of all social classes in a grand compromise.
Deviant action in general, and criminality in particu-lar,
became threats to the established order, the preservation of
which in its essentially existing form was a supreme value.
The state not only had to guarantee the rights of the individual but had to preserve the social order. The putative
needs of the society as a whole were paramount and the criminal
was socially responsible to the society and its state. In
theory the question of moral guilt was abandoned and the legal
question became the objective power of determining whether an
individual had transgressed the moral consensus of the community embodied in legal formulations and, if so, what measures
ought to be taken to prevent further crimes and protect
"society" (Radzinowicz 1966: 52-53).

Punishment was not only a moral retribution for willfully
inflicted wrong, but also a means of social defense by which
society protected itself from its criminals. Just as the
question of guilt became less a moral category and more an
objective category of jurisprudence, so too the question of
punishment became one of the objective assessment of the best
means to protect the social order. The norms of society were
granted general validity from which it appeared to follow that
attempts to coerce individuals to readjust to these norms were
justified.

With the advent of the social sciences, and within the
premises of positivism, there was an increased potential for
developing rationality. Undermining the metaphysics of the
religious view and the free will assumptions of the classical
school, positivism was an advance because it focused attention
on empirical processes, in particular the social environement.
The attempts to understand criminality often focused on such
observed deficiencies as a lack of education or technical
skills, or inappropriate habits. While in the early crude
positivism, criminality became merely a conditioned mechanical
response to these objective factors, there remained the implicit possibility that the criminal could be brought to understand what had "gone wrong". In practice this self-understanding was considered irrelevant since the information was
usually monopolized by official decision-makers who, with this
knowledge, would then attempt to manipulate the individual to
alleviate his short-comings. While there was an expanded potential for the criminal to understand his "crime", this was not
the key to the reformation--the prisoners became an object for
social science manipulation. More fundamental questions such
as why what was defined as "stealing" was wrong, were irrelevant under the assumption of the legitimacy of contemporary
legal norms.

As positivism emerged as the dominant approach in criminology there was an accompanying shift from the "custodial prison" to the "progressive prison" (Gill 1962; Rothman 1980). The development occurred in the context of social movements of reform in response to the negative social effects of rapid capitalist industrialization. By 1870 a National Prison Association had been founded in the United States and an International Congress on prison reform had been founded in London (American Correctional Association 1966). Among the Declaration of Principles of the American Association were such reforms as the indeterminate sentence, parole, probation, classification and diagnosis--the gamut of early rehabilitation (Murton 1976: 9-10). Penitentaries were still justified on the grounds that they provided deterrence, but the negative conception behind the silent system was replaced by the imposition of more "positive" experiences which would assist the criminal to return to society a transformed man.

Elmira Reformatory for men, which was opened in New York in 1876, advanced reformation as its explicit aim, systematically adopting the principles of parole and general education for the prisoners. This reform programme was applied uniformly to all prisoners and the failure of the reformatory is often attributed to this application of "mass treatment" which ignored the individual needs of each prisoner (Murton 1976: 11). The application of common standards was, in turn, explained by the lingering influence of the classical tradition with its emphasis on certain and equal punishment and the trend towards positivism was viewed as a growing awareness of the individuality of prisoners and the need to tailor programmes to identifiable needs.

Despite the development of a reform ideology and the implementation of specific recommendatins in some prisons, there were few concrete applications of the principle of reform before the 1930s in either the United States or in Europe. The Archambault Report (1938), which describes conditions in Canadian penitentiaries during the 1930s, indicated that little improvement had occurred since the early days of prisons in Canada. The institutions then existing were described as being very old, with idleness, strict discipline, the rule of silence, corporal punishment, poor classification, unsatisfactory education and no worthwhile trades training as regular features. Prisoners remained in cramped cells 16 hours of every day. They took their meals in their cells and were allowed a mere one-half hour exercise period a day. Ill-trained staff, poor medical services and no planned recreation programme added to the miserable conditions. No newspapers were allowed inside and writing and visiting rights were highly restricted. Only one set of regulations existed for all types of institutions with a total of 724 possible offenses, many of them trivial, for which prisoners could be punished within the prison. The internal trials were described as unfair and as allowing no appeal. Corporal punishment could be administered in Canadian prisons at a time when it had been abolished in The United States.

There was virtually no classification of inmates for differential treatment, as the habitual, young and often mentally incompetent were housed together in one institution. According to the Archambault Report, any classification that had taken place was designed for security reasons rather thasn for reformation (: 104). The regulations for classification of prisoners, which had been devised in 1899, had not been implemented. The number of prisoners employed at productive labour was also very low. Hours of work for those who did have productive tasks were low, which meant long hours of enforced idleness. Although prison farms had been in existence before Confederation, management was inefficient and prisoners' pay so low that there was little incentive to work.

It was not surprising, then, to find that prisons were in various stages of unrest. Between 1925 and 1936 twenty disturbances occurred in prisons across Canada, ranging from mild rebellions and work stoppages to violent confrontations which involved serious damage to the cells and assults on guards. The inmates who participated in these disturbances were prosecuted and received corporal punishment and often additional sentences.

At the time of the Archambault Commission, 72% of the prison population consisted of recidivists (Superintendent of Penitentiaries 1937), a proportion which is similar to that found today. At that time prisoners were released in a suit of badly-fitting clothing with $10 prison pay. The Report of the Commission attributed this to the absence of treatment inside the prison as well as to the conditions they faced upon release. In the words of the Commissioners, the alarming increase in the recidivism rate was caused by "the absence of any serious attempt to effect the reformation of the prisoner while he is incarcerated...and...the failure to provide him on release with adequate assistance to enable him to obtain honest work and support himself and his dependents" (: 249).

The primary punitive nature of pre-positivistic criminology had not been superseded. On the contrary, it continued to shape the contours of the North American Prison system although it was supplemented by more sophisticated versions of positive penology. The further extension of the refomatory concept in the twentieth century was based on the empirical finding that, relative to the total population, those confined in prison had less education and fewer marketable skills. The implication was that these deficiencies were environmental factors which drove individuals into criminality, and consequently educational and vocational training, carried out in a coercive setting, would logically undercut the necessity to commit more crimes. Criminality might still be rooted in sin and sloth, but these had environmental causes. Penitence and hard work alone were insufficient unless prisoners could be returned to society with more employment skills and better options than they had previously. Crime was seen as a social phenomenon related to specific conditions within which the causes of criminality could be sought. The contours of mid-20th century debate on prison reform were oriented around the poles of individual rehabilitation versus individual punishment--liberalism versus conservatism.

CHAPTER THREE

LIBERAL AND CONSERVATIVE CRIMINOLOGY

Conservative Criminology

The most primitive motivation for punishing an offender was the desire for revenge and retribution. A retributive philosophy, which dominated the thinking about the method of handling persons convicted of crimes, continues to provide one pole for the contemporary ideological debate on corrections. While those who emphasize retaliation as an acceptable response generally operate within a classical conception which stresses the deterrent effects of suffering and certain punishment, the general theoretical perspectives which have contained this element justifying a law and order approach have varied over time.

In the first half of the twentieth century, retribution was couched in a body of ideas which Gibbons and Garabedian (1974) refer to as "conservative penology" (cf. Farris 1955; Barnes and Teeters 1951). Generally, conservatism is less an academic and more an official response. The authors counterposed this set of ideas to a "liberal" view which emphasized corrections and rehabilitation. The process of ideological change in corrections has been very complicated and any simple division between liberal, conservative and radical theories can not do justice to the varieties of responses. Nevertheless, as two opposite poles on a continuum of response, the emphasis on punishment which generally characterizes the conservative orientation as opposed to the more liberal concern with reformation, suggests that these general divisions have some conceptual utility. At different times, greater or lesser emphasis has been placed on one of these alternative responses. While the advocates of each view strive to meet their own objectives against that of the competing philosophy (for example, more guards versus more vocational training), our primary concern is with the basic assumptions on the nature of corrections which the two dominant perspectives share. For all their tactical differences concerning the implementation of changes in the prison, they remain within a more general common framework.

Conservatism and liberalism are relative terms. What at one point may appear as a radical new theory may later be seen to have consequences of a conservative nature, in the sense of acting to preserve the status quo (cf. Zeitlin 1981: 58-60). The rhetoric of the "new right" in the west is profoundly conservative despite its themes of possessive individualism and competitive capitalism, which at one time were thoroughly liberal if not radical in the context of the period. In this sense, conservatism pre-dates liberalism which is is a relatively more recent ideological phenomenon, although "reforms" have an ancient lineage. Conservatism, then, stands generally for a society of inequality which is presumed to be legitimate. It is supportive of the status quo, and with respect to criminality stresses the differentiation of the evil and the good.

Contemporary critical theory assimilates conservative ideology and the development of functionalism in the nineteenth and twentieth centuries. While functional theory had profoundly conservative consequences in many of its forms, there is also a liberal version of consensus theory. The right-wing version would suggest that there is only one proper form of ideas and behaviour and that it is the duty of the elite to enforce these standards on others. With respect to modern conservative theory, which had to come to grips with the liberal revolution, conservatism reflected a viewpoint on society which claimed that the social order was composed of different parts, all of which functioned together like a living organism. The social organism was harmonious and rational, and this rationality was embodied in the corpus of social laws and priorities which guided human conduct. Not only was society seen as institutionally sound, but it was assumed that it could be studied as an integrated whole in which people occupied different positions but the majority of them held fundamentally similar values. The process of inculcating the values of society was not automatic, however, and it was possible that certain individuals would not exhibit these shared and rational views. Such people were the deviants and defectives, and it was the task of social institutions to bring these people to accept or at least comply with the consensus.

Along with other existing institutions, the prisons were accepted and justified as being necessary for the protection of this great commonality. As in the liberal perspective, specific problems were recognized. But what distinguished the conservative viewpoint was its greater degree of commitment to the existing forms of institutional structures and the emphasis which was placed on the application of negative sanctions.

Within the perspective of conservative criminology, the ideological position which distinguished between good and bad people was cast in a new mould to suit the changed circumstances. Deviants in general were defined as social misfits who violated the values held by the respectable majority. Criminals were, by definition, out of line with the society as a whole--they were an aspect which was foreign to the culture rather than being a specific social product. Since the existing social order was deemed both just and rational, those who violated the law had acted against the interests of society, against their own supposed real interests and ultimately against reason itself. In this way the conservative perspective, when carried to its logical conclusion, tended to link individual responsibility for criminal acts with irrational behaviour (Gordon 1974); criminals then had to be isolated in preventive detention.

The question became whether in principle, criminals could understand the norms and come to accept them. The link with rationality suggests that the appropriate conservative response should have been educative, unless it were in fact denied that criminals could come to a reasoned acceptance of what were seen as common values. It is this denial which, in part, underlies the connection between conservative viewpoints and the application of negative sanctions, although the primary motive remains retribution and revenge. In the conservative view, for various reasons of a personal or individual nature, whether these be genetic or characterological factors such as a "natural sloth or indolence", criminals could only be coerced to conform to what were held to be mainstream values. Only by inflicting suffering could the degenerate be forced to submit. The conservative emphasis on punishment follows logically from a consensus view of society when the deviants are deemed incapable of coming rationally to accept the dominant values, Prisoners become objects for social practice rather than beings capable of rationality. They possess free will enabling them to act contrary to the social order, and consequently punishment is appropriate. In opposition to this emphasis on the perversity of human nature and the acceptance of the status quo, rationality was the watch-word of liberalism where originally it spelt rejection rather than acceptance; critique rather than faith. In an historical irony, the emphasis on rational human action is currently a cornerstone of the conservative perspective which assumes individuality responsibility and cupability.

This conservative viewpoint characterized many early American sociologists who, as social pathologists, tended to focus their essentially descriptive analysis on what they conceived to be the margins of the society. The study of "criminals, juvenile delinquents, prostitutes, drug addicts, the physically defective, the mentally ill and the poor" was conducted within an individualistic perspective which implicitly condemned deviants as essentially marginal and blameworthy. The consensus framework adopted a "kinds of people" approach to deviance (Reasons 1975).

Liberal Criminology

A number of alternative conceptions of crime have been placed under the rubric of "liberal criminology" (eg. Taylor 1984; Ratner 1984) and counterposed to conservatism. The general category of liberalism included psychological theories emphasizing psycho-dynamic deficiencies, environmental theories focussing on social and economic deprivation (with roots in 19th century Marxism), as well as explanations concerning the

creativeness of individual deviants. While the differences in
these views may have been at least as great as their simi-
larites, they shared a concern with the reformation of individual offenders. Modern liberal criminologies has been more
critical of the status quo but still accept as valid the basic
institutional features of the social order, although liberals
place more importance on imperfections and inequalites within
it. A certain degree of injustice is admitted in social distribution which is considered at least partially responsible
for creating criminality (Gordon 1974: 70). Consequently in
contrast to the conservatives, liberals tended to take institutional reform more seriously. Nevertheless, a distinction was
drawn between those aspects of society which could be changed
and those which were necessary for society in general and
therefore unavoidable. For example, it was argued that substantial inequality in rewards for different occupations might
be an essential feature of all societies, but this did not mean
that actual poverty was necessary. The only reasonable response, from a liberal viewpoint, was to implement pragmatic
and piecemeal reforms while continuing to assist those agencies
and institutions, including the police and prisons, which were
attempting to provided public protection.

Mid-century reform minded criminologists adopted an opti-
mistic prognosis from the principles and methodological
premises of positivism. In the liberal view, crime was a deri-
vative phenomenon arising from social strains which were rooted
in the social structure itself, rather than a shadowy excre-
scence apart from society. Despite this emphasis, which undercut to some extent the full responsibility of the actor for his
criminal actions, criminality was still regarded as a characteristic of certain indivǐduals. Consequently, the search for
the causes of criminality took the form of seeking the motiva-
tional factors which were specific to criminals which distinguished them from the law-abiding majority. Among these
"liberal-cynical" criminologists, Gibbons and Garabedian
(1974:53) cite Sutherland, Cloward and Ohlin, Cohen, Sykes,
Cressey and Merton.

This multi-causal approach, when combined with the study
of marginal groups in society, gave rise to the view that there
was no single criminal sub-group. Rather North American
society was characterized by a plurality of sub-groups, and
social norms operative in specific social contexts may be
contrary to those of other groups. Criminals were those who
belonged to criminogenic sub-cultures in which they were
socialized into patterns which were contrary to those of other
majority groups. Democratic ideology held that the norms of
the majority were reflected in laws and the rights of minorities would be protected only insofar as they were compatible
with these dominant values (Cohen 1955; Cloward and Ohlin
1961). Crime, then was primarily a characteristic of the poor
and was linked to the existence of a counter-culture generated

by deplorable social conditions which necessarily produced human beings deformed or deficient in certain ways. Crime was the active manifestation of these conditions (Wright 1973: 7n, 17n).

The concept of deviance, then, underwent some modification while a dominant, if not general, societal consensus was still assumed. The adoption of a pluralistic perspective, however, made the concept more relativistic: behaviour which was normative for one group may violate the prescriptions of a second group and be considered by them to be deviant. It seemed that the application of the label of deviant was not instrinsic to the behaviour in question, but depended upon the particular context from which the act was viewed. This pluralistic view did not explain, for example, why the norms or values of one group should be defined as criminal in the society, except by an implicit acceptance of the democratic version of the consensus viewpoint that the majority was correct, and that law reflected the views of the majority. Both of these assumptions were later to be called into question.

Consensus Theories and Punishment

Fundamentally the conservative and liberal views share certain basic asusumptions about the supposed normative structure of contemporary Western society and the need for "social defence" (Rothman 1980). The concept of deviant behaviour served on the one hand to legitimize those whose social conditions of existence predisposed them to adopt social norms which were taken to be generally valid for society as a whole and on the other hand, served the moral function of discrediting other modes of behaviour. With this viewpoint, both the mode of conduct and style of life of the normative majority and those of the various deviant minorities were all shaped by the social structure--a structure which included both universal features assumed to be common to societies in general and specific historical antecedents, all of which were essentially out of the control of individuals in any of the positions in the social structure as a whole.

The conservative perspective had served to legitimate the social structure by universalizing its features and by uncritically accepting its political ideology. The consensus viewpoint negated any conception which postulated specific social classes or groups as in general responsible for social problems, and focussed attention on blameworthy individuals. If substantial inequalities were indeed crucial to the existence of a social structure as many liberals argued, and criminal behavior was consequently endemic to society, the amount and seriousness of crime was a function of the degree of inequality. It followed that crime could be mitigated by the conscious intervention of social institutions--in particular, the state--to try to ensure that, as far as possible, unjust inequalities were eliminated. In this sense, the liberal view-point at first addressed itself to lower class deviance--it was still an attempt to explain the differences between law-breaking and law-abiding citizens (Thio 1975: 277-278).

Liberal perspectives seek the causes of crime in a compli-cated combination of structural and psychological factors which are, however, susceptible to conscious manipulation to alle-viate the strains. It does not escape from the conservative emphasis on individual motivation; and, in recognizing social causation, it seeks the cause of criminality less in basic structural inequalities, and more in inequalities of distribu-tion and the behavioural aspects of these inequalities which can be manipulated without raising any larger questions. For example, one solution suggested was that family planning among the poor would reduce the size of families and result in fewer people living in poverty (Jones 1965 cites Kerr 1958 and Spinley 1953). The social problems perspective isolates speci-fic social institutions from their place in the larger social context and addresses the question of readjustments within the currently existing arrangements.

The conservative criminologist differs from the liberal principally on the focus of attention. To the conservative, social institutions are fine; the question is simply the prag-matic one of trying to adjust the individuals to the normative order. For the liberal, while the institutions in the society are given general validity, specific imbalances are noted, and the efforts at reform are directed both at attempts to ration-alize the institution, and to reintegrate individuals. Ulti-mately liberal reformism is couched in terms of the most efficient means to adjust individuals to the social system. Both are types of consensus theories (McDonald 1976) and rest on a social problems perspective which directs attention to questions of individual inadequacy and malintegration.

The acceptance of the liberal viewpoint undercuts some of the justification for punishing social deviants and brings to the fore the possibility of transforming social conditions, within the narrow confines of causality accepted by such theories. In practice, however, the emphasis has been on transforming the individual manifestations of these conditions. In other words, consistent with the liberal view--within the consensus framework--is the concept of treatment, or "rehabili-tation". It is not surprising, then, that the development of the rehabilitative model in corrections arose concurrently with the ascendency of a consensus theory in North American soci-ology during the relatively prosperous post-war years. It is not only a punitive approach that is intrinsic to the consensus theoretical framework (McDonald 1976: 25).

The usual debate between punishment and treatment is in this sense a false one, not only because both emanate from a

single theoretical outlook, but because both are merely alternative strategies for an identical social goal. In this perspective the object of the socialization process is to incul-
cate what are thought to be prescribed social norms and values.
The deviant becomes by definition one who has failed to
internalize these normative patterns. Having demonstrated
social inadequacies or inappropriate behavior, the deviant is
subject to corrections which means attempts at resocializaton.
The question of whether punishment or treatment--the former
implying the imposition of purely negative sanctions, the
latter implying the more constructive application of programmes
designed to resocialize in a more positive manner--is to be
advocated, is based purely on the pragmatic grounds of what
works, what is successful in achieving the goals prescribed by
the consenus model.

The integration in varying degrees of both aspects--
punishment and treatment--in the liberal conception of corrections follows from the basic legitimacy which is granted to
what are deemed to be general social norms, the criminal law,
and ultimately the state, but elements of past models are
incorporated. The conservative view was not simply superseded;
on the contrary the dominant motivation of punishment has its
source deeply in the roots of the pre-classical period. The
liberal model, as was suggested above, did not supplant so much
as supplement the earlier philosophy. But within this mixture
of views the proportion of emphasis placed on negative or
positive aspects is not static or unvarying but rather is
subject to changing emphases related to the specific historical
situation. The crucial questions are those of the fundamental
aims of the correctional process: whether in their own terms
rehabilitation is a serious objective or whether, despite the
rhetoric and implementation of reforms, the administrators of
the prison system remain fundamentally wedded to a punitive
philosophy.

Reformation and Training

The first fruits of positive criminology identified the
existence of significant objective deficiencies in the prison
population which distinguished them from the hypotheticl
average citizen. The low educational level, lack of technical
training, insecure employment, and so on were assumed to be
causes of criminal action--the concrete manifestations of
social inequality which at one level were slowly being
ameliorated by state action. Coupled with this was the need
for a more direct intervention on an individual level to solve
those problems which had already been developed and were manifest in the criminals themselves. During this early period the
theoretical emphasis was placed on objective processes; there
was less emhasis placed on the social psychological aspects
such as individual motivation, which were to under-gird the
full-blown ideology of rehabilitation.

Rehabilitation refers to the process of attempting to re-socialize individuals to comply with social rules considered to be valid by the agency responsible for the conversion. At its most basic level it necessarily assumes that people can change and that identifiable individuals or groups of individuals are in need of such changes. The medical model will be considered to be a particular type of rehabilitation which rests on specific theoretical and philosophical grounds. Its particular defining characteristic is its foundation in individual pathology and its emphasis on psychological mechanisms in the causality and "cure" of criminality. Rehabilitation in general assumes that criminals are distinguishable from non-criminals who are considered to be normal, and, further, that it is possible to change individual criminals through training programmes or psychological processes to make them law-abiding citizens in the absence of institutional changes.

It is this emphasis on the individual psyche which especially characterizes the medical model of rehabilitation, although it has often appeared as one component in reformation schemes. By and large, rehabilitation is a 20th century phenomenon, although it has deep historical roots. This view of crime as being like a disease undermined the view that the prisoner was responsible for his actions, since the medical model assumed that criminal acts were caused by endemic psychological problems. Unless these basic problems were resolved, then the ex-prisoner would return to criminality. The deviant behaviour, then, was not the source of the problem, but only a symptom. This medical model is usually counterposed to a behaviouristic view which asserts that the criminal act itself is the only problem and the internal psychological source of criminality is, at best, irrelevant and, at worst, illusory. By rewarding "good" behaviour and punishing "bad" behaviour, the criminal will gradually learn to do "good" automatically. Both of these views, of course, still assume that the correct approach to criminality is to change the individual deviant.

The modern approach to criminality rests on the foundation of earlier psychological explanations. The religious and classical models took into consideration elements which might be termed "motivation"; and the religious component of prisons, which existed from its origins, administered to the criminal's mind in the name of the soul. In the nineteenth century Canadian penitentiaries, prison chaplains were diagnosing prisoners according to psychiatric notions and personality defects. It is the official recognition of the rehabilitative ideal and the attempt to institutionalize its concepts which demarcates the post-1945 years as the period of rehabilitation. In this period the ideology was given official legitimacy and consciously advanced as the basis for a reform of the prisons.

The rehabilitative model of corrections, which became among many liberal criminologists the most common rationale for

imprisonment, has most succinctly been summed up by the concept
"training" (Hawkins 1974: 101-102). It implies the practical
imparting of vocational skills which are expected to enhance
the market opportunites of the ex-convict, and also carries a
moral connotation which refers to the resocialization of the
prisoner to values and attitudes assumed to be linked causally
with non-criminal behaviour.
Prison education, then, should "have a central concern with
ethics or morality" and aim at inducing an attitude change
among prisoners. Essentially this means movement towards de-
layed gratification--"the keystone of middle class morality"
(Duguid 1981: 434).

This notion of rehabilitation is also linked with the
social conception of crime and particularly with the liberal
view that criminal action is, at least to a degree, socially
caused. From a view of the criminal as being determined by one
specific factor, characteristic of nineteenth century positivism, the attribution of causality changed to a series of
factors which were salient to a greater or lesser degree. The
contradiction between social causation and individual responsibility was addressed in such a way that, in general, humans
were responsible for their actions, but "will" was, to a
degree, conditioned socially. That is, criminals had had concrete options and could have freely chosen to act lawfully or
unlawfully. They had chosen the latter and the issue was
defined as a re-conditioning of the will so that upon their
release ex-prisoners would choose the law-abiding path.

The view prevailed that criminals had to be removed from
their social situation which was continually reinforcing their
criminal choices, to an institution in which they would learn
to abide by legal stipulations. It was thought reasonable,
however, to distinguish between prisoners according to the
extent to which their will was amenable to change. There were
still those defined as incorrigible whose will to commit crime
was unchangeable. Those relatively new to the status of felon
were thought unlikely to be fully consolidated in their criminality and specific features of the environment of the prison
were expected to reverse their desire to break the law.

The general philosophy behind this reformative model has
been clearly spelled out in Britain. As expounded in the First
Rule (1964) of the British prison system, "the purpose of
training and treatment of convicted prisoners shall be to
establish in them the will to lead a good and useful life on
discharge, and fit them to do so". (Quoted in Hawkins 1974:
102). Reform was simply "the substitution of the will to do
right for the will to do wrong" (Fox 1952: 72). The issue was
one of ideas, of values and attitudes, aspects which perhaps
were not susceptible to precise measurement but were crucial to
affecting real and permanent changes. The will to do right
became a mysterious internal phenomenon and changing it re-

quired very personal influences: it was a "deliberate and very personal growth" (Fox 1952: 72). It was taken for granted at the time that the prison provided the necessary external pre-requisites for individual reform as well as real opportunities. As institutionalized in the British system, the philosophy of reformation reflected the strong influence of the classical tradition, intermixed with psychological theories.

The Medical Model

The medical concept of rehabilitation derived more directly from the liberal tradition which postulated the exis-tence of "sick" sub-cultures. It was based on an explicit medical model of criminal behavior which defined criminal ac-tion to be a form of psychological illness. While originating in the deprivations of lower class life, the psychological problems assumed in the medical model were supposed to be cured in the prison--that is, with even a greater degree of depriva-tion and degradation. Emphasizing the process of first diagno-sing the illness, then prognosticating and employing logically consistent treatment, the search for the cause of criminality did not extend beyond the prison walls (as though criminals were a random sample of those who committed illegal acts).

The "rehabilitator" was charged with inducing a deeply-rooted personality change in the individual, a fundamental change in the prisoner's self-conception, rather than merely a surface compliance to the rules and the order imposed by the officials. It was maintained that the symbolism of social ostracism and rejection which were indicated in the act of being condemned to prison would tend to undermine previously maintained values and thereby open the possibility of subse-quent resocialization which would involve the reconstruction of new values on a presumably non-criminal basis (Wheeler 1971). The consensus view of society did not contemplate a situation in which the act of imprisonment itself is conceived to be an unjust imposition of sanctions by a powerful group upon power-less individuals whose existing values would be reinforced by the experience. The basis would then be laid for a more funda-mental rejection of the social system of which the prison was a part.

The transition from one dichotomy to another--from con-ceptions of the criminal as being evil to being sick--which occurred with the ascendency of the medical model in the 20th century in the case of ordinary criminals, paradoxically was slower and met more opposition for those persons convicted of drug offenses. Prior to 1930 the Narcotics Division of the U.S. Treasury Department, regarded the drug addict "as a self-indulged pander to his own evil appetites instead of a gravely sick man." The addict was an "immoral, vicious social leper, who cannot escape responsibility for his actions, who must feel the form of swift imparted justice" (Reasons 1974: 144-145).

In the case of drug offenses we can see the close connection between the belief in individual responsibility and the legitimation of the application of primitive sanction. The contradiction between the justification of punishment and the social causation of criminality is resolved by denying the efficacy of social processes. During the 1950s, while criminologists were suggesting the implementation of rehabilitation within a consensus framework the older criminal model continued to mould legislation dealing with drug offenses, providing for no probation, and for more severe and inflexible penalities, directly connected with the responsibility imputed to the addict for his condition. Addiction was itself defined as a crime, and the addict, along with sundry other "deviants", "was characterized as ... violent, degenerate, un-American [and] an enemy to society" (Reasons 1974: 147). The result was that in the decade following World War Two the jails and prisons were increasingly used to punish addicts and users, all denied alternative treatment. By the late 1950s, however, the medical rehabilitative model was being advanced by both the legal and Medical Associations, which advocated the establishment of experimental out-patient clinics for addicts based on the view that addiction itself was an illness susceptible to cure. The classical model, then, imputes individual responsibility and responds punitively, while the medical model, substitutes pathology and advocates treatment.

The rehabilitative model in prisons has its roots in the late 19th century and involved a substantial reduction in the conservative emphasis on the evilness of criminality. The viewpoint of the social pathologists who had delved into the seamy underside of respectable society tended to condemn deviants less as evil and more as moral incompetents. Once it was assumed that criminals were pathological or sick, individual psychological treatments were required in order to cure those criminogenic tendencies which were amenable to social influence (Bishop 1974: 97). According to the California Department of Corrections: "Crime is certainly in part a mental trouble. We...hope that prisons are becoming more like hospitals". Since prisoners were psychologically "sick people", "psychopaths", "mentally disturbed" (Evans 1980: 37, 1, 72), their cure required the skilled implementation of the techniques of psychology: diagnosis and counselling, and the full use of the so-called healing sciences of psychiatry and social work (Murton 1976: 27). The full development of the philosophy of rehabilitation within the consensus theoretical framework reflected the relatively prosperous 1950s, the time of the Great American Celebration. Post-war prosperity not only provided the material basis upon which it was possible to implement some institutional reforms, but also provided the basis for a theoretical analysis which could assume a dominant social consensus of liberal values to which the errant prodigals in the prison could be returned. The assumption that ordinary prisoners were mentally disturbed, the application of the "sick" label, deprived individuals of their integrity (Arboleda-Florez 1983: 47-48; Opton 1974). The psychiatrist became the chief ideologue within the prison walls, the successor to the 19th century chaplain. As practiced in the prisons, psychiatry had disciplinary and punitive implications (Powelson and Bendix 1951). Sullivan (1980) claims that these "helping professionals" operate behind a mask of love while acting as state control agents.

Rehabilitation involved not merely the task of developing job skills, but also altering the attitudes and the psyche of the prisoner. It is based on the premise that criminals were drawn into unlawful behaviour by particular situational factors (Hartjen 1974: 132) which had left a more or less deep imprint. There was a basic supposition that, despite these social liabilities, law-abiding options were open. The crux of the matter in the rehabilitative philosophy rests on the individual's need to develop a recognition of his own objective and subjective liabilities, and then commit himself to strategies to overcome these. But the essential point is that this is viewed within the context of the individual re-adjustment to social values which are assumed to be general in society. The problem was less the objective situation itself, and more the subjective orientation of the individual to the situation (Hartjen 1974). The possibility opened by social science of developing an understanding of social processes within which criminal activity could be explained had been transformed into an inquiry into individual deviance. By focusing on the individual manifestation of social processes, rehabilitation carried the individualization of criminality one step farther.

CHAPTER FOUR

FUNCTIONALISM AND THE PRISON

We have argued that sociologists in the 1950s, building on the work of the social pathologists and searching for the causes of criminality, developed an increasingly sophisticated theory of deviance. Although accepting a generally consensual model for the social order as a whole, sociologists paid increasing attention to the existence of deviant sub-groups. This implied that the social isolation of members of these counter-cultures in the confines of the prison would potentially strengthen rather than weaken the deviancy. The medical model's increasingly specialized "knowledge" about psychological processes tended to make the convict an object of scientific intervention. Rehabilitation, however, was threatened because prisoners were not merely objects but acting subjects who could not only resist the "cure" but could actually contract a worse dose of the "disease" in the prison itself. In the field of penology, sociologists applied their functional framework to a study of the social organization of the prison in order to understand the process by which prisons apparently increased rather than decreased criminality.

The functionalist view of criminality recognized that what were defined as criminal actions were generated by social processes that were an integral part of the operation of society. From this fact it was concluded that criminality was a "social fact", that it was endemic to society as a whole and necessarily functioned to reinforce social values; a society without crime and criminals was, then, a theoretical impossibility (Durkheim 1958). It was not incumbent on criminologists to question how "crime" was created and defined by social processes, nor did they dispute the general legitimacy of existing social institutions. Their concern was to discover the processes by which the society generated criminality in the hopes that subsequent intervention could lead to the control of this phenomenon and deflect potential criminals from this path.

Among the significant approaches with social policy implications which were devised in this period, two deserve special mention. Sutherland and Cressey (1974) developed the concept of differential association, implying that criminals were socialized in deviant sub-groups. Merton (1938) sought the source of criminality in the disparity between general social goals and unequal access to legitimate means. Some people were not in a position to obtain by legal means the things the society determined to be worth owning and therefore, to obtain these generally desired goods, they had to resort to innovative and often criminal actions. Both theories had programmatic implications and were reflected in the concept of "training", in both its moralistic and vocational aspects. Either the prisoner's values could change to become consistent with the majority, or his skills could be enhanced giving him a better chance in the labour market upon release (greater access to legitimate means). The programmatic consequences of these potentially useful theories of the "middle range" reinforced the liberal attempt to resocialize the malintegrated. Merton's theory, in particular, further implied the need to devise schemes of redistribution to minimize the inequalities and hence decrease criminality. When Merton postulates that crime as one form of deviance results from a lack of legitimate channels to reach socially defined goals, he is describing how criminal behaviour is generated by a social structure of a certain type. His analysis does not explain the structural basis of this malintegration of means and ends. Rather Merton concentrates on how social values in a competitive society breed law-breaking behaviour among the disadvantaged and relatively advantaged alike.

The attempt to specify theories of the "middle range" had the positive effect of focussing on social causation and implying the need for social change, albeit of a piecemeal fashion. A more directly empiricist strand in liberal theory rejected this theoretical approach and the institutional reforms which were implied, and declared that the development of criminology had been retarded by the illusory search for causes. The days when sociologists could seek the general causes of criminality were declared to be over; the medical model was taken to an extreme and it was declared that, since it was ludicrous to seek for a theory of disease, to seek for a theory of criminality was equally a chimera. Walter Reckless, for example, rejected the concern for the search for causes and advocated instead the "realistic and comparative study of criminal behaviour" (Grygier 1965: 154). Abandoning sociological approaches, this school of criminology advocated a form of behaviourism and practised "decision theory" by which was meant the scientific administration of the correctional system (:155). Social scientists were to use their expertise to assist the prison officials in the running of the system. This theoretical outlook assumes significance as a scientific covering for a return to a primary emphasis on control mechanisms in the prison. In the present context of the assumed failure of the rehabilitation model, this approach to sentence management has become increasingly popular among prison administrators and some criminologists.

If the search for the causes of criminality had kept sociologists in the ivory tower, the adoption of decision theory moved the social scientist squarely into the Warden's office. This approach leads directly to an extreme empiricism, the advocates of which disdain to waste their time by discussing some of the more controversial issues in penology such as how crime is defined and by whom, and takes as its function the pragmatic attempt to determine the most efficient way of achieving the goals of the prison. That is, it must implicitly assume answers to these questions and its value neutrality is nothing but the acceptance of the dominant ideology. It is here that "grand theory" conducted within a consensus framework, and empiricism, which ignores theoretical questions, can be seen to arise from one identical ideological position: the pragmatists merely assume the essentials of the theoretical basis elaborated by the theorists.

During the 1950s and early 1960s there was not only implicit acceptance of the legitimacy of the social goals which institutions such as the prison were designed to serve, but acceptance of these institutions themselves as the best instruments to achieve the goals, albeit with various alterations which only they, the social science experts, could suggest. The larger issues having been shunted aside, it could then be claimed straight-forwardly that: "If criminology is to have any practical application, it must lead to a scientific control of human behaviour" (Grygier 1965: 155; Mannheim and Wilkins 1955).

Decision theory may be regarded as the increasing development of more sophisticated methodology to answer a narrowing range of questions. Whether the ultimate goals of rehabilitation had been attained could not be measured, precisely because it seemed impossible to operationalize the concept of "will" and the notions of profound personal and internal changes which were bound up with the philosophy of rehabilitation. These mysterious inner changes were declared to be, at best, unscientific. Since the presumed inner state of the rehabilitated man was regarded as outside the realm of scientific discovery, recourse was taken to the outward behaviour of the criminals which could, it seemed, be directly observed and understood.

Particular attention was focused on the question of recidivism: the proportion of released convicts who are reincarcerated. It was argued--based on the assumption that criminality was an individual problem--that the idea of rehabilitation had, as its major goal, the transformation of a criminal into a non-criminal. Various ideas might abound about what makes a person a criminal in the first place, but irrespective of the assumptions which underlie the intervention, and the nature of this intervention, the acid test was whether the individual was able to "go straight".

Recognizing that the ostensible aims of rehabilitation involve such concepts as increasing self-understanding, developing personal relationships, as well as learning respect for authority (Hood and Sparks 1970: 171), criminolgists rationalized the use of recidivism as the crucial measure of success by assuming that staying out of prison would be the practical outcome of these impossible-to-measure factors.

Without being able to explain the precise causative chain which
prevented an ex-prisoner from being re-convicted, this fact
alone was taken ipso facto as evidence of rehabilitation.
Decision theory did not reject the philosophy of rehabilitation
so much as assume its major tenets. The problem was redefined
as one of attempting to measure the effects that differential
experiences in prison would have on behaviour. The goal of
rehabilitation was to produce a change in attitudes rather than
simply external and short-term compliance. This internal qual-
ity was difficult to observe, so the pragmatists in prison
administration assumed that failing to be re-convicted was a
change of behaviour (as if there was only one independent
variable) and that this change in behaviour could be an indication that some change in attitude had taken place. In practice
the question of assessing the consciousness of prisoners became
irrelevant and the emphasis was placed totally on compliance.

The use of recidivism as a measure of treatment success
tends to be problematic. First, not being reconvicted does not
necessarily mean that the ex-prisoner remained within the law.
It could simply mean successfully avoiding recapture following
subsequent acts defined as criminal. However, it remains true
that, compared with those who have no previous record, the odds
are against ex-prisoners avoiding reconviction. Second, subsequent conviction may be for a considerably less serious crime,
although all reconvictions may look the same on paper. More
importantly, the treatment programme may not be the most in-
fluential factor in determining whether individuals "go
straight" upon their release. Compared with the very real
problems of finding worthwhile employment, decent housing,
reestablishing family ties, and so on, the treatment undergone
in the prison pales in significance (Hood and sparks 1970: 177-
185). The trend, then, was towards an increasing methodological sophistication as prediction methods became increasingly
individualized to take account of the numerous disparities
which have to be taken into account for successful manipulation. From rather crude random sampling techniques, the tech-
nicians of social science developed individual matching (Wilkins 1958: 201-209), and more complicated base expectancy
tables (Mannheim and Wilkins 1955). From these beginnings the
methodological precision has developed further (Gibbons 1963;
MacNaughton-Smith 1966), often divorced from some of the larger
problems of theory construction.

While in the optimism of the 1950's it was uncommon for
social scientists to question the existence of some social
institutions, it was understood that they were in need of
reform of a kind which their expertise could offer. The research perspective was put into practice in the prison to
assess the efficacy of existing programmes. Ultimately the
effect of this research was to provide ammunition for those
interested in undermining the philosophy of rehabilitation. It
was found that the various programmes made very little differ-

ence in reducing recidivism. Functionalism, then, assumed programmatic significance in corrections during the reform current associated with post-war prosperity; with the end of prosperity and the associated debunking of functionalism, various forms of behaviourism (existent for a long time) have now filled the theoretical breach by acting as a validation for a return to first principles--control and maintenance of order-- in the prison. This argument will be elaborated below.

The Prison as a Social System

An important direction taken by criminologists who operated within a functional framework was to examine the prison as a social system. While these writers began their research with the assumption that existing social institutions were appropriate and necessary, they questioned whether they were fulfilling their purposes. Social scientists began to study the social structure of the prison, divorced from the society of which it was a part. An early major work in North America on the sociology of the prison came out of the Chicago School in 1940. Donald Clemmer's The Prison Community (1940) applied to the prison the conception that human action was a functional adaptation to environmental forces (Morris 1965: 70).

Studies of penology which have utilized a functional framework have tended to emphasize two aspects of the social structure of the prison: the types of roles which the prisoners themselves adopted in the prison, particularly the rules of conduct devised by and for the inmates, and the characteristics of their unofficial leaders. The first aspect, the "inmate code", was seen by Clemmer as the internal form of social control among the inmates. In this view, this code of conduct attempted to institutionalize solidarity among the prisoners on one hand, and consolidate anti-institution values on the other. Unofficial leadership in the prison community was generally accorded by the prisoners to those who best exemplified the tenets of the inmate code and who were most consistent in anti-administration values. Clemmer noted, however, that there were widespread violations of this code in practice and that only flagrant breaches were controlled by the other prisoners. The process of acculturation to the norms of the inmate code was termed "prisonization", a process which was determined by the degree of contact with "hardened" prisoners (Wheeler 1971: 98). To the extent that this anti-administration solidarity actually existed, the problem of disorder was endemic to the prison. However, since the point of understading was the scientific control of behaviour, this knowledge was expected to form the basis for rational intervention.

In Clemmer's work, as well as the studies conducted by Clrence Schrag, the main concern was the problem of power and authority. The essential problem with the straight-forward custodial prison was that there was virtually nothing but dead

time. The situation, at its most simplistic, was that hundreds
of men were confined in an institution and subject to significant deprivations against their will, while a second group of
men were designated to maintain order.   Despite the formally
powerful position of the authorities in the prison, if the
prisoners valued non-compliance above all, even the routine
functioning of the institution was problematic.   In the custodial prison there were mostly negative sanctions, and, as these
were progressively used, the store of possible sanctions
dwindled.   As punishment becomes more severe, then the lessen-
ing of this suffering as a "reward" might become more appeal-
ing.   As the maximum punishment was reached, there was little
to deter more serious breaches of prison discipline.   Internal
order had to be maintained in a situation in which systematic
brutality on the part of the administration was increasingly
illegitimate.   To the extent that some concrete reform proposals were heeded by the prison administration, and corporal
punishment outlawed, the problem of social control potentially
intensified.   Coupled with this were the state of prison conditions and the problem of over-crowding.

        An increase in the incidence of prison rebellions in the
early 1950s in the United States resulted in part from the
accumulation of these long-standing problems.   It became abun-
dantly clear that the prison system was not working.   Some
attempts at reform had been initiated in the United States with
the creation of a central federal department in 1930, however
the effect of the depression and the war had been to continue
the process of ignoring prison reform.   The sudden intensifica-
tion of prison rebellions as well as the uncovering of numerous
cases of what was defined as "maladministration" of the prison,
had the predictable result: much more attention was given to
correctional problems (McGee 1972: xv).

        In Canada there were few prison disturbances in the early
post-war years, and none between 1948 and 1951.   In the early
1950s there was a substantial increase in the number of people
incarcerated and the resulting tension contributed to the out-
break in 1953 of a number of significant prison rebellions.
In 1954, destructive rioting occurred at Kingston penitentiary
and, by official count, one hundred prisoners out of a total
population of 600 participated in a disturbance at Saskatche-
wan Penitentiary in 1955 causing fires and considerable damage.
Sentences were meted out to those assumed to be ringleaders.
In all official reports, rebellious prisoners were described as
psychopaths and as being mentally disturbed (Commissioner of
Penitentiaries 1955).

        During this same period there was a dramatic increase in
disturbances in U. S. prisons.   Between 1950 and 1953, there
were 50 major riots, making this the most disruptive period in
the history of U. S. prisons (McCleary 1968: 130).   Prior to
this date, the years with the most disturbances had been 1929

(fourteen) and 1937 (nine) (Fox 1956). These rebellions were spontaneous outbursts against conditions which had come to be regarded as intolerable and many reforms were demanded by the prisoners in the course of the rebellions. These included reforms in the day-to-day running of the prison and were also aimed at specific practices. According to Pallas and Barber, however, they did not dispute the legitimacy of the social order: "They challenged the abuse of power rather than its nature." These authors argued further that the rebels were largely co-opted by the trust they had in the rehabilitators (1976: 240-241), as the dual interests of prison reform and prisoner reformation overlapped.

Prison disturbances are an endemic part of the system although like any rebellions their specific timing depends on many circumstances. Such periodic episodes take many forms, as they do in the larger society, and include individual manifestations such as fights and destruction of property as well as spontaneous collective acts of disobedience (Bukhart 1979: 361). Large-scale prison disturbances have one salutary consequence: they bring conditions within the prison to the attention of the media and the public. As for any oppressed group the repressive conditions themselves are only a necessary underlying cause of overt social rebellions. Very oppressive social conditions can be associated with social stability.

It has been argued that prisons in the 1940s were tightly secure and authoritarian (Ignatieff 1981: 158). Within these conditions, a practice described as a "semi-official form of self-government" (Desroches 1983: 180; Hartung and Floch 1956) gave inmates of some prisons a degree of implicitly tolerated control over certain aspects of prison life. The post-1945 bureaucratization of the prison undermined this understanding as staff members took over the control of a wide range of activities, often in the name of rehabilitation. As officials wavered ambivalently between controlling and reformative policies (Douglas et al. 1980: 201), some of the privileges and some of the informal power yielded by prisoners were revoked (Sykes 1958). When the American Prison Association concluded that the causes of rioting were within the prison system itself, the implications of the report were reformist; the failure to implement prison reforms had brought the predictable rebellion. The fundamental causes cited were: inadequate financial support, official and public indifference, sub-standard personnel, enforced idleness, lack of professional leadership, excessive size and overcrowding of facilities, and unwise sentencing and parole practices.

It seemed that nothing had changed in a century. The reforms proposed in the past had not been implemented partly because of political conservatism and the retributive ideology of the prison administration. Liberal reformers continued to argue that, with sufficient money to support the appropriately sized army of social and welfare workers, all problems could still be solved within the present system. Post-war prosperity provided the basis for this view and the resources for the implementation of some programmes.

There was still the rather troublesome question of inmate solidarity and the view that prisoners were a consolidated mass with anti-administration sentiments. The 1950s rebellions seemed to provide substantiation of the view that the prison was indeed a powder-keg which needed very little to set it off. The question of the maintenance of order was essentially the question of power, and social scientists began to look further into the essential power relations within the prison.

Social Roles in the Prison

An important theoretical statement of the problem of power in prison was formulated by Gresham Sykes (1958). While it has frequently been his typology of argot roles within the prison which has been the focus of academic attention, his major contribution was their application to the analysis of the problem of social control. Sykes makes it clear that prison is not simply a question of the physical environment, but is undergirded by an ideology--by a philosophical rationale--and that this must be understood in order to comprehend the social system of a prison. He enumerated the ideologies of imprisonment as punishment, retribution, deterrence and reform, and suggested that the prison was attempting to fulfill contradictory goals. In particular there was a major contradiction between the "value or priority attached to the maintenance of order as opposed to a possibly competing objective" such as individual reformation (:17).

Sykes' approach to the social system of the prison adopted an "organization viewpoint" according to which the guards and administrators were concerned less about either punishing the offender for past wrongs, or for rehabilitating the prisoner to prevent future crimes, but rather were concerned with internal order, the smooth running of the institution. This pragmatism was then surrounded by a theoretical justification couched in the phrases of rehabilitation. At the level of every day activity the staff possessed a formal monopoly over the legitimate means of coercion--a situation Sykes termed "total power". The rise of the penitentiary in the 1800s had meant breaking the inmate community which had existed among prisoners and substituting formal control mechanisms by the administration. The effect, however, had been to drive the culturte underground and to draw a sharp and antagonistic demarcation between prisoners and keepers (Ignatieff 1978).

The crucial problem of power in the prison, as Sykes saw it, arose from the problem of legitimacy in the institution. Sociologically, power based on authority combines two elements:

the legitimacy of the wielders of power to exercise control, and "an inner, moral compulsion to obey" (1958: 46). Social organizations derive their strength from both of these aspects. Prisoners, according to Sykes, did not at that time dispute the formal legitimacy of the prison. The prison hierarchy consisted on the one hand of gradations of staff, who obeyed orders because they thought that they should, and on the other hand a mass of prisoners under little moral compulsion to obey. Rather than responding out of a moral sense of duty prisoners had to be "forced, bullied, or cajoled into compliance" (1958: 47).

For Sykes, force must remain the ultimate sanction but recourse to violence is only appropriate in extreme situations of unrest. Focusing on the prison as a social system he recognized the necessity of other less obviously violent measures of social control, despite the formal existence of "total power", in order for routine functioning: "A blow with a club may check an immediate revolt, it is true, but...will be of little aid in moving...inmates through the messhall in a routine and orderly fashion" (1958: 49).

If punishment cannot be used to maintain orderly functioning, Sykes was quick to point out that in the maximum security prison, the store of possible rewards was greatly minimized. Fundamental to the regime of the prison were specific deprivations which eliminated the ability of the staff to reward compliance. With the ability to coerce prisoners curtailed by the limits inherent in the use of punishment in the prison, at least for everyday activities, with no development on the part of the subject population of any inner moral compulsion to obey and with virtually no rewards with which they could "bribe or cajole" prisoners into the imposed social patterns of conduct, the prison faced a paradox of control.

It was in this situation, argued Sykes, that a system evolved in practice which allowed the prison to exist in some equilibrium. This was the corruption of the guard. Essentially Sykes meant that the guard had to permit some behaviour, normatively defined as criminal, to occur in the prison, in return for some general compliance on the part of the prisoners. This does not suggest that all guards actively participate in this activity, for example by smuggling in contraband, although some do. Rather it indicates an informal license for some prisoners to exercise internal control over others.

Thomas Murton has exaggerated this into what he terms the "fiction of prison control" (1976: 65). By this he means that the amount of power exercised by the guards, ultimatly, is equal to that granted by the prisoners. The degree of official control exercised in the prison will vary from prison to prison and from time to time, but the ultimate sanction lies in the hands of the state and its armed forces. According to Murton, the free community would not tolerate open prisoner control, which is what he claims exists, and consequently the fiction of staff power is maintained as being advantageous to both groups. Here Murton translates the response of a formally powerless group to try to manipulate its circumstances and ameliorate some of its worst conditions, into actual power. The two must not be confused, and both are distinct from the potential power which prisoners have in the possibility of solidaristic opposition. Relative to the coercive agencies of the state, however, this potential power is itself precious little unless linked with wider social movements.

In his analysis of the rebellions which took place in the New Jersey prison in 1952, Sykes disputed the common "powderkeg" theory which inferred that the prison was always on the verge of rebellion. The freedom accorded the prisoners to operate their own small social world was conducive to control. However, it always contained the potentiality of over-stepping the bounds set by the system. At some point, the attempts of the prison leaders to exercise power conflicts with that of the guards and, consequently, physical coercion is applied temporarily. Rebellions, then, are endemic, but they develop as a cyclical process.

Concentrating his analysis of the informal structure on argot roles in the prison, Sykes distinguished between those individuals who played "cohesive" roles--meaning those who supported the staff and had a vested interest in stability-- and those who played "alternative" roles. The former, he maintained, were kept in line by the informal rewards made possible by the definition of limits of permissible behaviour in violation of prison rules. The imposition of strict discipline, however, undermined the functioning of the informal reward structure, and created a situation in which "alienative role players will displace the cohesively oriented inmates as the foci of power and authority within the inmate group" (Morris 1965: 75-76).

The crucial questions of social control addressed by sociologists concerned these types of roles in the prison social system and the question of leadership. Sykes' study suggested that rather than there being an inmate code which, in general, solidifies prisoners in opposition to the guards and promotes "anti-social" elements to leadership positions, there are compliant prisoners as well who, with judicious distribution of informal privileges, can be counted on to maintain control. The process of turning a blind eye to activities defined as illicit, encourages the development of exploitative roles in the prison--it has the effect of dividing prisoners and allowing many matters of control to be handled by the prisoners themselves, not as an equal body, but as a group with informally defined leadership.

The recognition of the inverse relationship between punishment and inducement hierarchies implies that while the use of maximum sanctions precludes the threat of more severe measures, it also makes inducements more attractive. The notion of a hierarchy of inducements suggests that the greater the deprivation the greater the efficacy of positive control measures. The practical working out of these hierarchies leaves much room for complexities. One significant practice used to control prisoners in the system who have little further to lose is a second type of guard corruption: the development of means of social control in the prison which are formally defined as illegitimate. Corporal and capital punishment have been legally barred; but the application of such coercive measures, up to and including the use of "hit squads," restores some of the power of the guards based on arbitrary punishment. Here we encounter the phenomenon which in one Canadian institution was nicknamed the 'Mafia'. The guards have access to both legitimate and illgitimate means of coercion in the prison. They can confine prisoners to cells, call security inspections at night, delay meals, all as attempts to harass inmates (Parliametary Sub-Committee 1977: 43-47). Acts of harassment are also directed at recalcitrant staff members. The report of the House of Commons Sub-committee on Penitentiaries describes a guard as being partly responsible for a major rebellion at Millhaven. It says: "The eruptions and violence were born of anger, frustration and oppression within the tight and unnatural confines of prison over unresolved grievances transfers, harassment and provocation".

Although typically prisoners udergo what Goffman termed "self-mortification" upon entering the prison for the first time (1961), what are described as new identities quickly emerge. These are not all identical because of a combination of prior learning and different treatment and experiences. Just as the rehabilitators are right when they complain that prisoners do not automatically accept absolute responsibility for their imprisonment, so too do they not all equally condemn the institution. Prisoners' self-concept, which had been dependent on their position in the social world outside the prison, is transformed through their contact with the inmate society (Tittle 1972; Homer 1981). Since this process does not imply that all prisoners develop an anti-administration attitude, the result is an increased opportunity for official control through selective manipulation of prisoners.

Clarence Schrag also disputed the thesis of general solidarity among prisoners and devised a categorization of social types in prison. He suggested that the inmate code, as postulated by Clemmer, did exist, but only characterized one possible role among many taken by groups of inmates. There were some roles in the prison which were completely antisocial, as well as some prisoners who preyed on others and prisoners who adopted the codes presented by the prison administration. This

46

description not only was more realistic in its depiction of the
effects of the prison regime, with its hierarchy of inducements
and punishments, but provided a theoretical basis for intervening to support the distinctions. This means, first, encouraging compliant prisoners by a reward structure within the
bounds of prison practice defined as legitimate; and second,
justifying segregation of troublesome prisoners who are inter-
fering with the "best interests" of the majority of prisoners,
and third, ignoring certain practices within the prison itself
which encourage the development of a hierarchy of exploitation
within the prison population.

As a causal element to explain the failure of the prison
regime to be effective, Schrag emphasized that more attention
should be paid to these various relationships among prisoners,
given that leadership seemed to be exercised by those he described as "criminally mature" and "least improveable", whose
status was enhanced by "psychoneurotic or psychopathic behaviour" (Schrag 1971: 85-90). His research efforts were
directed towards the identification of leadership types "so as
to promote the eventual prediction and control of leadership
phenomena". As Schrag puts the case: "Detailed knowledge of
the general characteristics of leaders and of the variations in
leadership preferences among different groups of inmates should
facilitate the prediction and regulation of interpersonal con-
tacts and influences within the prison community. Such information should simplify the control of the prisoners by means of
segregation" (85-86). Schrag's data tended to show that prisoners chose as leaders those with similar characteristics to
their own, with regard to number of convictions, length of
sentence, and so on. The finding that, in general, inmate
leaders are those most opposed to the prison regime, is explained by the predominance of multi-timers with more consolidated anti-administration views. The conclusion drawn from the
study is "the utility of segregation as a device for regulating
inmate interaction" and neutralizing the ability of the "criminally mature" to corrupt others. This argument was designed
to oppose the existence of large prisons with diverse populations, proposing that more specialized institutions be constructed.

Studies of the prison social structure also have implications for a reformative prison management. The existence of
leaders who espouse values antithetical to the regime of the
prison--including correctional programmes--is thought to be one
significant limiting feature which prevents actual rehabilitation from taking place. Empirical studies have found that
those prisoners who most clearly articulate the code of ethics
associated with prisonization tend to oppose participation in
programmes designed to resocialize values and attitudes (Quinney 1970: 179). The attempt to manipulate the "social climate
and the leaders" would result in breaking up of the "gangs" and
enhancing "positive groupings" (Grygier 1964: 173). The role

of the professional staff becomes the studied observation of the prison population for the purpose of intervening in the functioning of the inmate system ostensibly to counteract nega- tive aspects which detract from the treatment being provided. Thus, when T.P. Morris agrees that prisons can be made more effective social systems but then argues that "it is yet to be recognized that more efficient prisons in which staff morale is high and staff-inmate conflict minimal can prevent men return- ing to crime" (Morris 1965: 86), he argues as a criminologist who, at least formally, takes to goal of rehabilitation seri- ously. Of more practical value to the administrators is the need to keep close tabs on the prisoners' interaction in the attempt to maximize the probability of compliance. The key to efficiency is peaceful co-operation, and the policy of inter- vening in the social system of the prison achieves the purpose of maintaining control and is rationalized on the assumption that a "happy prison" may be a reformative one. On these grounds a reformative prison is utopian unless people can come to enjoy being punished or enjoy soul-searching transformations of personal character.

Control or Rehabilitation

By approaching the study of the prison from the point of view of isolating it, as a social system in itself, from the wider society of which it is a part, two distortions in partic- ular are produced. As with decision theory, there is an impli- cit acceptance of the institution and the larger social struc- ture. This leads to the negation of any fundamental questions concerning the role of the prison in the particular society. The prison is not a deserted island upon which Robinson Crusoes have been cast who must construct a new world (which in any event will still reflect the world from which they had come originally). Sykes implies that he is not at all interested in these questions: you have a prison, the problem is to study it. The point is that this stance precludes understanding institu- tions in general and prisons in particular.

The second distortion arises in the very concept of a "prison community" which is a contradiction in terms, Orwellian in its implications. One must locate the prison in its place as a coercive instrument of social control within the larger context. It is not a society by itself but a means of punish- ment, and it is seen as such by the prisoners. Power is not something that merely is held in abeyance, to be used to put down disturbances--the position of being a prisoner is one of continuously and pervasively being coerced by an external power. The prisoners are not there because they want to be but because they are being punished. Being not only in a situation of being powerless, but of being actively punished, minimally through a confinement maintained by specified agents, the re- sponse of prisoners to their situation is based on this sense of oppression. You cannot separate what goes on inside a prison from the question of what a prison is.

Prisonization, or the acculturation to the social system of the prison, was assumed by penologists to be a bad thing and not a realistic response to a condition of oppression. In their attitude to this "code" and the leadership which espoused it, the social scientists exposed the ideology behind their work. The conceptual leap was taken from defining that such a culture, with anti-administration attidues, exists within the prison, to the assumption that its nature is "criminalistic". As Clemmer explains: "The phases of prisonization which concern us most are the influences which breed or deepen criminality and anti-sociality and make the inmate characteristic of the criminalistic ideology in the prison community" (Clemmer 1971: 9). Here the irony of the whole concept of a "prison community" is fully exposed; inmate solidarity in the face of imprisonment is defined as anti-social, while overt manifestations of co-operation with the prison regime become symbolic of an individual having a "fairly stable personality", an adequate socialized relationship prior to incarceration, and a character strong enough to reject dogmas. Such a solitary man, who forms no social attachments of any commitment with prisoners, shows "a willingness, under certain situations, to aid officials, thus making for identification with the free community" (Clemmer 1971: 94-95).

The functional viewpoint, which begins by isolating the prison, as a "community" in itself, from the larger community of which it is a part, in the end has to fall back on the assumption that, after all, the prison regime represents the "free community" and to be fully "social" the prisoner must identify with the outside, through its putative agents inside. Hence prisonization is defined as a process of becoming anti-social, and co-optation is seen as adoting the consensus view outside the prison. In this way the organizational sociologists studied the prison not only by isolating it from its social context but by assuming the legitimacy of that context.

If you leave the analysis at the level of the institution, prisoner solidarity is a reasonable response to conditions. From an administrative point of view, however, the degree of prisoner solidarity is seen as being in an inverse relationship with order in the prison. Although prisoners are placed in a formally powerless position, the strengh of prison rebellion rests in large part on their numbers, on the uniting of prisoners in anti-administration attitudes and actions. It is in the interest of prison administrators to attempt to interfere with the prison's social system, to the extent that it objectively exists and leads in the direction of legitimizing and encouraging prisoner solidarity. The study of prison leadership serves explicitly to achieve this aim. It is assumed that assimilation to the prison culture prevents identification with the regime (i.e. with free society) so therefore any intervention which disrupts the normative assimilation of prisoners is beneficial to them, to their own reformation, since it is held that the real interests of the prisoners and of the existing society are identical.

By studying the informal relationships between prisoners, the administration would be in a better position to reward selectively, and try to prevent prisoners with anti-administrative attitudes from achieving leadership among the inmates. Rather than simply a means of achieving greater control of prisoners, the study of the social system was set in the philosophy of rehabilitation, and the interest of sociologist in the prison was then justified in terms of this prevailing notion. The inmate code was based on the dichotomy between prisoners and guards--the oppressed and their oppressors --and emphasized solidarity among the former, at least vis-a-vis their common plight, and their attempt to negate the influence of the prison staff. In this sense the inmate system was viewed by penologists as a road-block to postive rehabilitation, and the focus on inmate leadershp was justified as an attempt to interfere in this process and undercut the general hostility to the regime which was assumed to be linked with the failure of individuals to reform.

What in fact ultimately occurs is that the necessity to maintain social control is formally justified as crucial to rehabilitation, and ultimately, as rehabilitation. The view that prison at least puts prisoners in a position to be positively influenced is taken one step further in the assertion that compliance with the prison regime itself is actual rehabilitation. The offender presumably had failed to develop the proper respect for legitimate social authority, and as a consequence committed criminal acts. In the setting of the prison he was to learn to comply with externally imposed power, and this compliance would then generalize to conditions external to the prison.

The administration, in whose interests it is to maintain an orderly prison, legitimates its attempt at control according to a crude behaviourism which does not distinguish beteen power and authority, but rather assumes that the disciplined meeting of externally imposed demands will, in some fashion, lead to following orders upon release. The transparency of this view is readily apparent. Its importance is in the recognition that, even at a time when the model of rehabilitation was on the rise, actions contrary to this philosophy had to be justified by coming under its general rubric. Control of prisoners and their rehabilitation become part of the same process.

CHAPTER FIVE

THE 'NEW DEAL' IN PENITENTIARIES

The attempt to reform the prison according to recommendations made in the 1930's was postponed for a decade and a half
until the post World War II years in North America. Relatively
more sophisticated efforts at classification came into
existence, vocational training was expanded and opportunities
for educational up-grading were increased. Many jobs within
the prison which had been assigned to prisoners and were necessary for the every-day functioning of the prison were redefined to be consistent with the rehabilitative philosophy and
were subject to more conscious distributional practices. They
acted as rewards for compliant prisoners and met the objectives
of the reformers since they appeared particularly good on
paper: many convicts could be shown to be participating in the
rehabilitation programmes in the prison. With the ascendancy
of the medical model, beginnings were made to introduce social
psychology and psychiatry to the prison with the development of
some types of therapy programmes. These reforms presupposed
the existence of indeterminate sentencing, classification,
training programmes and parole. These were part of the "new
deal" in the penitentiary system which was introduced in Canada
following similar practices in the United States.

These developments were by no means startlingly innovative
in the years surrounding World War Two. What was new was the
amount of resources available in the new welfare state for the
concrete implementation of the rehabilitative philosophy in the
prison system. We can distinguish between three types of
training programmes: first were those designed to rectify the
objective disparities which prisoners demonstrated relative to
the population. This meant the development of vocational
training and educational up-grading programmes which were
expected to give the ex-prisoner more legitimate job options
upon release. Second, programmes were developed to provide
constructive use of the prisoner's leisure time. The third type
was based on the assumption that social psychological traits
were associated with criminality. It was within the latter,
reflecting a medical model framework that the philosophy of
rehabilitation was most clearly manifest. The actual implementation of a wide range of rehabilitative schemes depended on
successfully determining the needs of the individual prisoners
and then matching them with appropriate programmes.

The introduction of a penitentiary programme directed
towards rehabilitation was given a very high profile by the
Penitentiary Service. In the words of the Committee on the
Remission Service (1956: 47): "Attention must be given to the
physical needs of the prisoner, his education and his voca-

tional or trade potential. The modern prison, therefore, must
be more than a mere place of human storage. It should, as far
as possible, be a place of worthwhile and creative activity".
The industrial programme was intended to have more of an emphasis on occupational training than on small work shop production
for institutional goods and services, as new industrial buildings were built and new machinery and equipment installed.
However, a look inside prisons in 1960 showed that only 38 per
cent of inmates were employed in penitentiary shops (Commissioner of Penitentiaries 1960). Fortanaro viewed the deadly
idleness and make-work projects of inmates as the most acute
problem inside the prison. In his words, "prisons have
developed a limited range of occupational activities that have
become almost a stereotype of prison programs" (1965: 312).
The image projected by prison officials did not coincide
closely with reality. Vocational training was supposed to be a
part of the work activities, but the vocational training
opportunities in institutions were limited. The Commissioner
of Penitentiaries (1960) reported 333 inmates enrolled in
training-courses, out of a total prison population of 6,344.
The same kind of misinformation seemed also to apply to
academic opportunities available to offenders. Few institutions offered sound programmes with qualified instructors.
Correspondence courses in many cases made up the whole of the
educational programme, since most institutions did not hire
full-time instructors.

The largest proportion of changes introduced in prisons
at the time occurred in recreation. According to Fortanaro,
competitive sports had come to represent the "new penology"
(1965: 313). There was an increase in professional services
such as counselling, chaplaincy, and psychiatric and medical
services which became part of the programme of treatment. The
total number of professional staff, however, was still very
small and special services were provided for only a small
number of individuals.

Classification

In the early history of prisons, all condemned persons
were housed together regardless of age, sex or health. Subsequent prisons were segregated along the lines of sex and age,
with certain prisons specified as adult institutions. The
most basic type of classification in the prison distinguished
between prisoners according to how dangerous they were thought
to be. In addition to this level of "dangerousness", classification also means the identification of specific individual
deficiencies. Within the rehabilitation philosophy, classification refers to the second of these, to the allocation of
specific types of prisoners to the separate treatment programmes according to identified needs. Classification of inmates
for purposes of treatment was first systematically introduced
in the United States in 1930 and four years later it was adopt-

ed by the U.S. Bureau of Prisons (Gill 1972). In 1947, the Penitentiary Service in Canada began establishing postitions for Classification Officers who would assemble information about prisoners to be sent to a Classification Board which would decide on individual treatment.

According to John Fortanaro, those activities formally described as classification consisted of alloting inmates to housing and work, with only a few institutions having anything approximating classification for treatment (1965: 309,310). He viewed the high ratio of inmate population to classification staff and the lack of qualified staff, as making it impossible to implement a proper classification. Officers with backgrounds in the military, police or security forces, or with a fresh B.A. were being hired. Segregation of inmates, that is, the practice of allocating different categories of prisoners to separate areas of the institutions or to separate institutions, seemed to be serving administrative and custodial expediency rather than rehabilitative goals. In Fotanaro's view, segregation appeared to be based only on age, length of sentence and criminal history. This still produced an undifferentiated and heterogeneous population requiring numerous treatment programmes.

The concept of classification for treatment rests on the premise that there exists differences between individual prisoners which are related to their type of criminality and that each prisoner requires differential treatment. This would involve a thorough diagnosis and planned programme of activity for each inmate. This, in turn, requires that a team of professionals as well as a varied and liberal set of treatment programmes be available in the prison. Classification was connected to the development of sophisticated behavioural techniques developed during the Second World War in an attempt to enhance the motivation of American soldiers to fight, as well as to the subsequent proliferation of personnel trained in psychological techniques following demobilization. The growing prosperity of the cold war years provided the economic basis for the utilization of these skilled professionals in the prison.

Theoretically the development of classification had as its origins the conception of the criminal as being undersocialized or inadequate, as having failed to develop certain normative social characteristics. Since at first these deficiencies were deemed to be relatively unambiguous--even the least detailed study of the prison population could not fail to note the objective disparity in education and skills-- classification was designed to be the scientific instrument whereby these deficiencies could be appropriately diagnosed. If the programme could not be tailored to fit the individual, the classifier would be in a position to direct the prisoner to the best available programme for overcoming his handicaps. In one

sense, the search for causes was not so much abandoned as being
futile, as assumed to have been completed. On this basis penologists proceeded to take remedial action. Classification became "the cornerstone...of any progressive and scientific
system of dealing with offenders in penal or reformatory institutions. It is an indispensable element of the fundamental
idea of individualized treatment" (Mannheim and Spencer 1949:
1).

Classification was put into practice by social science
staff in the prisons as a reform measure which, according to
the prevailing theory of criminality, was an essential pre-
requisite for the successful rehabilitation of the convicts.
There was an additional aspect to classification which was less
directly connected with the ideology of rehabilitation. One of
the perennial problems associated with imprisonment was idleness. Of course, in the ideology of the early prison, idleness
was in itself a bad thing, while work was a positive value.
But when the crucial question is not a concern for the well-
being of the prisoner but rather for the orderly running of the
institution, idleness--that is, idleness in the specific context of incarceration--seemed to be linked causally with rebellious attitudes and activities on the part of the convicts. In
this sense the diversification of staff to run programmes
served potentially to defuse the atmosphere and provided
activities which could be justified on rehabilitative grounds.
This was particularly true of the programmes designed to fill
the prisoners' leisure time.

Classification was equally--perhaps essentially--a device
to assess the security risk of the prisoner. There had existed
previously notions of a distinction between the amenable and
the incorrigible prisoner. This distinction was to be made
more sophisticated by adopting, on a more systematic basis,
means of assessing the prisoners' dangerousness which would
determine the degree of relative options open to them within
the prison. At the outset the classification of risk was based
on such criteria as the length of the sentence, previous record, convictions and age. Classification would then sift out
those who would presumably benefit from reform programmes and
those who were considered too dangerous and required closer
supervision. The specification of the degree of incorrigibility, or the security risk, also determines the access to relative privileges within the prison. Consequently both the
threat of increasing the grade of risk, and the possibility of
relaxing it, serve as potent control measures for the running
of the prison. It is used to punish unacceptable behaviour and
induce compliance; and the security risk is tied directly to
the chances of parole, one of the rewards of the system.
Prison authorities now assert that they have no accurate means
of assessing the degree to which offenders are dangerous to the
public.

The classification of prisoners remains a fundamental cornerstone of the prison system. It represents both a necessary device for social control and rehabilitation, and is an extension of the indvidualized conception of corrections which was the major thrust of criminological theory as applied to prisons. Beginning with the premise that the criminal was an individual who was out of step with the social consensus, the "cure" rested within according to the medical model which underlay the practice of rehabilitation. It was as though each prisoner had some form of "bug" which, through sophisticated medical-psychological treatment, could be cured. The basic theoretical questions about crime remained unarticulated, replaced by some vague conception that over a long time enough information on the systmatic patterns associated with classifiable "bugs" would be compiled to enable a number of pragmatic and useful "theories" to be developed. Meanwhile, the criminologist could get down to the essential task at hand, helping individuals to adjust to the prison and thereby curing them and presumably solving the problem of crime.

Maximum, Medium, Minimum

The crucial issue is the contradiction between control and treatment. Despite the subjective wishes of some of the social science reformers, the changes in prison administration were not usually implemented in a way which maximized the potential for treatment, but rather in a way which increased official control. The twin responses of coercion and inducement, which became institutionalized with the distinction between "treatment" and "custodial" staffs, gave the appearance of being two separate interests, one of which was supportive of the prisoners and the other of the prison administration. It was in this sense that some prisoners had demonstrated a degree of trust in the rehabilitators in the 1950s. This distinction provides some basis for the view of prison policy as a power struggle between separate interest groups, a pluralistic view which ignores the fact that the struggle over the means of social control is relative to the response of those to be controlled, and that in the crunch the liberal reforms are shelved.

In 1959 a Correctional Planning Committee was established to propose a programme stemming from the recommendations of the MacLeod Report (Gosselin 1982: 75). The policy, as it was developed by the Penitentiary Service, consisted of three main goals: instituting a better programme of staff training directed towards the goal of rehabilitation, developing a more "competent staff", and establishing suitable institutions for training. Over the next decade, the number of institutions in the Canadian Penitentiary Service grew to thirty-four. The Service embarked upon an expansion of medium and minimum security institutions not only to provide the necessary means for carrying out treatment, but also as a means of relieving the overcrowding in the maximums at that time, a situation caused

by a sharp increase in the prison population in the 1950's.
The security classification of prisoners distinguished broadly
between three types, to correspond with the major types of
prisons envisaged by the Committee. Maximum security risks
were thought to be dangerous and/or incorrigible; medium
security prisoners were not considered security risks in the
sense that they would not actively attempt to escape. Their
detention was described as "ware-housing", a term with custodial and punitive connotations which, while it negates the
supposed rehabilitative functions of the medium, more precisely
describes the state of affairs. The third type of institution
was designed for those described as minimum security risks, who
were usually near the time of their release.

In 1959 Canada's first medium security penitentiary at
Joyceville was occupied. The operation of two open-type minimum
security work camps for public work projects commenced that
year, the beginning of a major plan for the expansion of minimum installations. This type of facility was highly praised
for its treatment value but was also a method of quickly accom-
modating hundreds of inmates. In the following years two
maximum were "converted" into mediums, new mediums and minimums
were constructed, and some minimum security farms were added to
some maximums. A specialized institution for drug addicts was
built in 1962. By 1963, seven maximums, four mediums and
fifteen minimums existed across Canada (Commissioner of Penitentiaries). A Ten Year Plan (1963-73) of institutional
development proposed that each region have a regional reception
centre, a medical and psychiatric centre, maximum, medium and
minimum penitentiaries, a special detention unit and a community release center.

The reform intention of this classification had several
justifications. The security arrangements in the maximum
prisons had to be directed towards the type of prisoner conceived to be most dangerous, which meant that the possibility
of rehabilitation was severly curtailed because of the maintenance of strict control. This condition applied to those clas-
sified as medium risks, who were presumably capable of rehabilitation, but had not reformed in the past because the options
had never been available to them. Secondly it was thought that
not only had there been a failure to provide positive options
for those prisoners regarded as amenable to change, but the
mixture of prisoners with varying security classifications
placed relatively inexperienced criminals in a social environment dominated by "hardened criminals". The learning process
in the prison was one of acculturation to the "criminalistic
sub-culture" which would negate any rehabilitation efforts; the
prison would merely serve as a crucible for crime, a critique
of the prisons which extends back to their origins.

The original intention for building a medium prison was to
identify those criminals who were amenable to change, those who

had not learned the informal rules of the inmate social system with its anti-administration stance, and place them in a prison which had as its primary focus not simply ware-housing but genuine rehabilitation. Mediums were to provide quantitatively better facilities, more vocational training options, an expanded recreation programme, and more inmate/staff contact. Having supplied the necessary physical plant for the rehabilitation of prisoners, there were thought to be two other necessary pre-requisites for success: (1) the selection of suitable prisoners amenable to positive change, largely those with a history of only one major conviction, and (2) the restriction of numbers so that the treatment philosophy could be administered adequately.

These pre-requisites for success were subsequently violated. There are two formal criteria for eligibility to the medium security prison, corresponding to the two basic functions which co-exist in the rehabilitative model. The first arises directly from the definition of the prison itself, and those prisoners are eligible who are considered 'medium security risks': those who would not be considered dangerous to the public should they escape custody. They are locked up, then, not for the protection of society, but as punishment. The second criterion is related to the ideology of reform: a prisoner is supposed to have made some commitment to change himself by taking advantage of the active training programme that is provided in the prison. The prisoner was to have demonstrated to the staff that he was prepared to take a look at himself, since criminality was an individual question. The prevailing view among the organizers of treatment asserted that the medium security risk prisoner required a certain degree of freedom of choice, and it explicitly stated that the manner in which this relative freedom was exercised by the prisoner would be a partially determining factor in his eligibility for parole.

The continuing high rate of recidivism and the over-crowding of the cell blocks in the maximum prison led to the transfer of increasing numbers of prisoners to medium security facilities which fulfilled neither of the pre-requisites above. Medium security prisons were changed in practice from prisons in which "the most amenable" offenders could undergo rehabilitation, to stronger mediums with a larger population to which multiple repeaters would be sent, no longer on rehabilitative grounds, but purely for security reasons: they were expected to be more resigned to the prison regime and less likely to attempt to escape. While separated from those thought to be most dangerous, the problems which had been associated with maximums, such as tighter control and the criminalistic influence of those with multiple convictions, were reproduced in mediums. It was acknowledged by a senior staff member in the Penitentiary System that now there is little difference between mimimum and maximum prisons with the exception that the ratio of staff to inmates was smaller in the mediums, which were therefore less expensive to run.

If, from the point of view of maximums, the policy of more generally defining the eligibility for mediums may have temporarily helped the situation of over-crowding, it had the effect of removing from the population those individuals for whom some rehabilitation programmes might have succeeded. It had the effect of defining the population remaining in the maximums as dangerous, thereby increasing the legitimacy of tighter control.

While official government reports sought to give the most favourable interpretation of prison programmes, more talk about penal reforms rather than actual implementation occurred in this period. The implementation which was carried out was frequently sacrificed to administrative convenience and punitive goals. There is a basis in reality for the complaint of the liberal reformer that reforms had not been implemented as reforms--that they had never been given an adequate opportunity. This concern with the failure of implementation underlies Fortanaro's criticism: "In Canada, prison is a way of life in defiance of the basic principles of humanitarianism, of reason and indeed of civilization itself" (1965: 322). He called for more systematic research into criteria for classification, the development of special resources in institutions and more self-determination of inmates in treatment programmes. Other Canadian criminologists, such as Kirkpatrick, were urging with renewed vigour the acceptance of the concept of rehabilitation in the middle 1960's (1965).

If we look at the mood of prisoners during this period we find reportedly peaceful years marred by no disturbances from 1956-61. A major rebellion broke out in 1962 at St. Vincent de Paul, where 50 inmates were reported to have "gone on a rampage", setting fires and breaking machinery. Ninety per cent of shops were damaged as well as 200 cells, twenty-six inmates were wounded and one killed (Commissioner of Penitentiaries 1963: 4-6). In 1963, hostage-taking incidents occurred at the B.C. Penitentiary as well as at St. Vincent de Paul, the prisoners involved demanding transfers to other institutions. Charges were laid against the inmates once the uprising was quelled. The climate in the maximum prisons was particularly tense at the time because of the delay in transferring prisoners from the maximums to the medium prisons. Rebellions were associated with heightened prisoner expectations. At the time there were many indications that changes were to take place. For example, in 1963 death sentences were commuted in Canada and a moratorium placed on capital punishment. It seemed that the rehabilitation model was about to be taken seriously in the country.

CHAPTER SIX

THE MEDICAL MODEL AND THE THERAPEUTIC COMMUNITY:
A CASE STUDY

If educational and vocational training represent the practical core of the rehabilitative philosophy, the iodeological
core was closely connected with the medical model of criminality. In penology, this model takes two related forms with
respect to individual rehabilitation (Bailey 1966: 155). The
"sick premise" provides the basis for treatment in therapy
sessions which are conducted on a one-to-one basis with a
psychologist or social worker. The "group relations premise"
is a variant of this approach. Behaviour is regarded as a
function of group relations and the major variables in treatment processes are assumed to be "social status, role, significant associates, group identifications and the values and attitudes learned through and reinforced in these interpersonal
situations." The concept of a Therapeutic Community is concerned with the second of these. By manipulating group relations the programme attempts to replace "anti-social" with
"law-abiding" values (:155). In the words of the Fauteaux
Report, the prison programme "must involve an attempt to change
the basic behaviour, attitudes and patterns of the inmate.
This depends not only upon the professional services of
specialized personnel but on the atmosphere of the prison. It
is only by sustained and determined efforts in these directions
that imprisonment can be made to serve a reformative or rehabilitative purpose" (Commission on the Remission Service, 1956:
47).

The Concept of a Therapeutic Community

The Therapeutic Community was the most important institutional innovation arising from the adoption of the medical
model in corrections, which attempted to turn the prison into a
hospital-like institution. The concern of the rehabilitators
was with the psychological state of the prisoners, which was
seen as the source of their criminality. Rather than being a
private matter involving the prison chaplain, or later the
prison psychiatrist, the psychological deficits presumed to
characterize offenders were to be corrected using group relations principles.

The Therapeutic Community (TC) was to be a special unit in
the prison within which the inmate would learn interaction and
communication skills. With the help of the group leader and
the other participants, the prisoner was expected to begin the
process of self-examination. It was to be a very personal
learning experience, requiring a high degree of commitment to

the group and the programme. With a less rigid routine than
that found in the prison as a whole and increased staff/inmate
interaction, there was expected to be a diminishing of the
harmful aspects of institutionalization (McCabe 1980: 246). If
criminality was in part a mental trouble, then it followed that
it was not merely a question of the prisoner being in need of
treatment, but of his recognizing the need and then actively
proceeding to rectify it. Hence the rationale for the establishment of an admission criterion to the Therapeutic Community: the prisoner was to have demonstrated a willingness to
reform. At a minimum there was built into this conception the
view that rehabilitation was largely an individual matter, and
that the ultimate responsibility for using the facilites (and
hence for rehabilitaion itself) belonged to the prisoner.
Nevertheless at the outset the rehabilitative ideal seemed to
promise much more and its implementation, involving the con-
signing of public resources, was accompanied by expectations of
considerable success.

The key notion in the Therapeutic Community, and the
crucial issue in the prison as a whole, is power. The notion
of the TC was that it was possible to break down the hierarchical chain of command (at least in that one unit, one part of
the prison as a whole) and make it horizontal rather than
vertical. The idea was to have a separate idealized community
within the prison in which power could be diffused, and in
which respect and authority would rest with the group as a
whole. Inside the TC, then, there was to be participatory
democracy which would be institutionalized in meetings where
the prisoners would help make decisions regarding the running
of the unit. The philosophy of the TC asserted that each
member of the group was to exercise some degree of decision-
making and have some responsibility for the decisions that
affect day-to-day living. It was argued that if prisoners did
not share in making the rules they could not learn responsibility.

The key concepts in the TC lexicon were "self-determination" and "self-learning"--to learn through experience. The
ideal of the TC centered on the develoment of self-regulation:
the prisoners themselves would make the rules by which their
lives were regulated. To implement this self-actualization,
daily meetings were to be held, attended by staff and prisoners
and decisions were to be made collectively. The formal function
of these meetings was two-fold. Besides serving as the vehicle
of decision-making, they were also to have a therapeutic purpose. Personal matters relating to staff/prisoner relations, as
well as inter-prisoner relations, were to be discussed openly
and resolved through verbal conflict. In this way both trivial
matters and such serious matters as fights in the unit were to
be handled largely by the prisoners; and by discussing matters
openly and progressively in a more honest fashion as the
"trust" between the staff and the inmates deepened, real learn-

ing was to take place. The prisoners would learn to solve
their problems of getting along with others, an experience
which would be generalized to life outside the prison. The
principle of control in the TC centered around the concept of
"dynamic security" which was to be achieved through this staff/
prisoner relationship and through the involvement of the inmates in their own control. This concept was distinguished
from the high walls, guard towers and guns which constituted
"static security".

The Therapeutic Community in Springhill

The Springhill medium security prison, opened in 1967, was
the first of its type to be built in Canada. It was intended
to be a prison with an explicit emphasis on rehabilitation and
was designed for young prisoners who were undergoing their
first sentence of two years or more duration. Some individuals incarcerated for a second period were also included provided that they were considered by the classification staff to
be susceptible to the motivations required in a medium security
prison for participation in programmes thought to be reformative. Consistent with the evolution of mediums from rehabilitative facilities to places of confinement, however, the population has changed to include multiple repeaters and older
prisoners.

When it was first opened, Springhill incarcerated between
150 and 200 prisoners in three separate units of cells called
Living Units. These units were designed as two-story wings
branching off from a central control booth. There are six
separate blocks of cells, two on each floor. The lights and
door locks are controlled from the central booth and the blocks
(called "ranges") can be shut off either by bars or by heavy
sliding solid panels (riot doors) reaching from the ceiling to
the floor, all controlled from the central command post. The
fourth side of the central area is reserved on the bottom floor
for staff, and on the top floor forms a large common room. It
is here that the staff/prisoner meetings are held although it
is also used for recreation.

There are four of these buildings at Springhill, constructed separately. The prison itself is laid out like a campus,
with the living unit as a core surrounded by buildings housing
facilites for physical exercise, a building for occupational
training with a number of trade rooms, a dining hall/kitchen
facility and administrative buildings designed especially for
counsellors. There is a separate administration building outside the perimeter, which is secured by a high metal fence. In
contrast to the massive Victorian stone fortress perched omin-
ously on a hill that is the maximum Security Prison in the
area, Springhill is less conspicuously set off the road and,
with the exception of the towers and wire fence--which gives it
a concentration camp atmosphere--might be an industrial park.

There are now about four hundred prisoners at Springhill, in contrast to the smaller numbers sent there previously, giving rise to an over-crowding of facilities. The ratio of prisoners to staff is about four to three, with one-third of the staff employed as security, about another one-third as a maintenance staff and a final third as correctional staff who have security functions as well. There are 12 living unit (LU) development officers, and 60 LU officers for the Living Unit and Therapeutic Community, as well as about a dozen vocational instructors, and half that number employed in the educational sector.

Springhill is a relatively small Nova Scotian town which has received most recognition for its coal mines and its recent history of mine disasters. With the decline of the traditional industry, the prison is an important source of local employment, and much of the professional staff is drawn from the local region. The people in the town refer to the prison as "The Institution".

A basic component of the rehabilitative programme in Springhill is the vocational workshop in which various simple skills are taught. It seems that few prisoners maintain a serious interest in the programmes over the length of the course, which is relatively short, a fact which may be related to the lack of labour market opportunities outside the prison. It provides a means to keep the inmates busy in order to supply the staff with furniture, gun-racks, smoothly-running motor-bikes or cars, and other services.

The Therapeutic Community in Springhill was inaugurated in the middle of 1969, with the initiative coming from the parole and prison services in Ottawa. The idea was brought up at a conference of wardens about the end of 1968 by the Director of Springhill. The interest which the project received at the time is now attributed to the existence of an "unorthodox" official who was serious about implementing reform proposals.

The origin of the TC has been traced back to England in the 1940s with the rediscovery of "moral treatment" (Jones 1952), but the concept was directly borrowed from the United States where it had been implemented in California (Spencer: 14-15). In Canada the programme had been shaped during the year prior to its opening in negotiations between officials in Ottawa and senior staff in Springhill: the Director, Supervisor of Classification, Chaplains, the official responsible for inmate programmes, a psychologist, psychatrist and social worker. Prior to the initiation of the project, the staff of the prison were given staff training which included inter-personal relations sessions in small groups. The TC was part of the "sensitivity training" trend operative at the time, found in many institutional settings, although particularly in education.

The Director allocated 50 prisoners from the two Living Units to the Therapeutic Community by taking those in one work area and putting them in the new third unit. During the first week (described by staff as "chaotic" and "rough") meetings were held to explain the programme to the prisoners who had not been involved in the planning process. According to the staff, the prisoners demonstrated the greatest degree of interest in the "privileges" they expected to have relative to the other living units, that is, in the concrete benefits they would have in the new programme. To the staff this was perceived as not entering into the proper rehabilitative spirit and was described as the prisoners "wanting this and that". This is one of the crucial distinctions upon which the rehabilitation ideal foundered: between prisoners' demands for reform of conditions and staff attempts to "reform" individuals.

Now inmates volunteer for the TC and have to make application to the staff. A Living Unit Development Officer, and some Range Officers interview the applicant, and depending upon his record and the interview, either admit him or exclude him. Those prisoners with long sentences tend to be excluded on the grounds that the literature shows the maximum benefit to be achieved within 12 to 18 months. Those who have longer to serve have little motivation for complying with staff demands and, after a longer stay, prisoners apparently get bored as the distinction between the TC and the other units wane. One criteria for inclusion is the prisoner's motivation for coming into the unit--the verbal acknowledgement of the rehabilitation philosophy. Those described by the staff as "paranoics" and "border-line psychotics" are excluded to avoid detrimental effects on the programme, the other prisoners and the prisoner himself. There were also what was described as unwritten criteria that are associated with person management. For example, they try to maintain a balance between talkers and non-talkers. Prisoners have to agree to abide by the rules which were set by the prisoner themselves, such as not playing musical instruments at night.

The Therapeutic Community has fewer prisoners and more staff than the other units, attempting to optimize on the one hand the chances for rehabilitation, and on the other the possibilites of "dynamic" social control. The optimal number of inmates, given the design of the TC, is 60, since above this figure it becomes increasingly difficult to "manage". There are 16 Living Unit Officers, 3 more than in the other units; however the 16 are responsible for both day and night shifts. After 11 p.m. all doors to the outside of the TC are locked. This not only serves to maintain closer contact between the staff and prisoners in the TC, but also emphasizes the dual function of treatment and control.

A typical day was described as starting at 7:00 with breakfast or "feeding" as it was referred to by the Range

Officers. There are two shifts with two units at a time in the
dining hall.   At 8:15 the prisoners go to work locations, such
as maintenance work arising from the needs of the prison, or to
vocational training.   Between the hours of 11:30 and 1:00 there
is a meal break.   Prisoners then return to work until 4:30.
The prisoners in the TC, however, leave work for their daily
meeting at 3:15.   This amounts to one privilege of being in the
TC. Following the evening meal the prisoners are at leisure.

During the first six months of its operation, the TC was
in its initial phase of experimentation.   There was a tendency
on the part of staff to refer during meetings to decisions
which had been made higher up in the hierarchy, thereby tending
to undercut the appearance of self-management in the therapeutic philosophy.   For example, the decision to leave the cells
open 24 hours every day had been made in the planning period
with the consent of the Warden, and it was broached to the
prisoners by the staff as having this higher support.   The
question became how much decision-making was to be within the
province, first, of the TC itself (assumed to be a community of
prisoners and staff as equals), and secondly of the prisoners.

During the experimental first half year the staff attempted to relinquish their direct power in favour of relying
on their authority within the meeting, and relying on the
prisoners to behave in a responsible way.   What this amounted
to was the staff holding their power in abeyance (latent
power), and hoping to direct the meeting to achieve the aims of
the prison.   That is, as long as the prisoners stayed within
the bounds of the permissible, and took upon themselves their
own sentence management in what was regarded as a responsible
way, then the process could proceed relatively harmoniously.
If you start from the opposite premise that the basic interests of the staff and prisoners are antagonistic, then the
evolution of prisoner autonomy will develop to the point at
which the demands of the prisoners conflict with the desires of
the staff.   Ultimately a point would be reached when demands
from the prisoners challenged the amount of power held in
abeyance, that is, threatened the order of the prison by going
beyond the permissible. The period of experimentation involved
a process of testing the limits of the new relationship to see
how much autonomy prisoners could achieve as opposed to where
the limits of autonomy would be drawn.

The staff could not at first simply impose order but had
to somehow get the consent of the prisoners.   The inevitable
clash occurred, with prisoners becoming increasingly bold and
over-stepping the invisible boundary.   The prisoners tended to
view the new structure as a means for achieving reform of their
conditions, a process viewed by the staff as wanting to obtain
privileges without earning them, that is, without realizing
individual rehabilitation. This expressed the fundamental clash
of interests.   The treatment staff serves the prison in the

capacity of person management while claiming to serve the prisoner as rehabilitators. The basis of any prisoner/staff relationship which develops in the TC relates in part to the social class composition of the officers. Many are not college trained but often people who come from class backgrounds which are similar to those of the prisoners. While the question of power separates them, this common experience allows a degree of informality to develop in the social situation.

Within half a year in the TC the breaking point had been reached, when as described by the staff, the prisoners were suggesting things that were not "therapeutic". It seems that the "open" meetings were becoming criticism sessions in which particular staff members were verbally castigated by the prisoners--a breach of prison discipline with important implications but certainly within the theoretical concept of the therapeutic community as a group sensitivity session. This process is quite predictable, for the first exercise of free expression by an oppressed group always concerns the conditions of its oppression which are directly linked with the actions of individuals functioning to maintain these conditions. At this juncture the Community could not be entrusted by the administration to manage itself and the latent power of the staff was "activated". Five or six of the prsoners deemed to be the leaders were removed from the TC. In the vocabulary of the prison staff, this was a "power group" which points to the crucial issue at stake.

The attempt to draw the lines in a non-authoritarian way had failed and the power of the staff had to be re-asserted. From the point of view of the rehabilitation ideology, this was a break in the system which had held out the prospects of increased autonomy. For the prisoners the re-assertion of the basic guard/prisoner relationship reinforced the perspective that the TC, at best, provided them with access to some privileges which were not granted to other units. The crucial power question had been decided in favour of staff. For the next period, in contrast to its ideals, the TC was run on a more or less autocratic fashion. This was a period of consolidation in which the limits were reinforced. Once the relative sphere of prisoner autonomy was clear, in what areas they could make decisions, then the TC began to run more smoothly from a staff point of view. According to the staff, the law is laid down infrequently and then is usually couched in an indirect way by following through verbally in the meeting the inevitable consequences which will follow the continuation of a certain line of conduct.

A resolution is then asked of the prisoners. The staff attempts to show concern, but there is always a threat behind it and the issue is then discussed and resolved in favour of staff. The use of the latent authority, in the words of the staff, requires skillful and subtle application. Drastic puni-

tive measures are avoided by essentially threatening a withdrawal of privilege. The process involves a degree of leniency
with petty rules in the give and take of an unequal relationship. This is what is meant when the administration describes
the TC as more relaxed than the other units--it is the sense of
relative privilege deriving from a less strict applcation of
some of the petty rules of harassment.

The meetings in the TC were originally scheduled to occur
daily on week-days but this has been changed to three: on
Monday, Wednesday and Friday. The reason for this was explained as the outcome of a conflict between two rehabilitative
schemes: the time spent in the meeting took away fom the time
spent on vocational training, and consequently the inmates were
not getting sufficient hours for certification. It also happened because the meetings (described as the "core" of the
programme) continued to degenerate into what the staff termed
"gimmie sessions" in which various grievances were put forward
over such issues as food, visiting rights, and so on. This
type of meeting was typical of the meetings at the opening of
the TC, during which prisoners voiced their complaints and
subjected the staff members to what was termed "scape-goating".
The problems of administrating such a large group--all inmates
meet at once, although many drift away and some do not show--
were partially resolved by the creation of some organizational
structure. A chairman and secretary were appointed and a unit
member's desire to speak was to be signified by the raising of
a hand. No agenda is drawn up beforehand, although items left
over from the previous meeting are raised again. A member of
the staff became the first chairman for the first time but
since then this role has been held by a prisoner. The areas in
which prisoners have some control include such things as determining the hour which the unit canteen is open, and whether it
should be open to prisoners from other units. The limited
supply of items for sale pressures the prisoners to exclude
other units, although some arguments are raised which are based
on a perception of prisoner solidarity.

All Talk and No Power

The basic contradiction in the TC is that between the
interests of the staff and the interests of the prisoners. The
philosophy of rehabilitation maintains a distinction between
the punishment and the rehabilitation of the prisoners and
appoints separate staff to each function. The security staff,
strictly speaking, have a custodial role and their contact with
the prisoner is an instrumental one of the "keeper". They are
formally charged with maintaining order in the prison, a process which is not always "static" security. One of the persis-
tent myths of the prison service is that the degree of freedom
inside the prison is directly proportional to the strength of
the perimeter. Presumably if prisoners cannot escape they can
do what they like inside. This is hardly the case and the

actual direction of the relationship is the reverse. The security staff are directly in charge of inflicting punishment, which in the first instance means maintaining the incarceration-- imprisonment itself being a punishment--but includes other control measures such as solitary confinement.

In the ideal world of the rehabilitative philosophy the treatment staff is different from the guards and is supposed to have the same "real" interests as the prisoners. That is, the prisoner's main interest is to get out of prison and not come back, and the treatment staff is to provide the expertise to guide the subjective development of the prisoner to the point at which he will become law-abiding. One principle aspect of this contradiction is between the actual subjective understanding of the prisoners and that imputed to them by the rehabilitator, who, in order to be succesful, had to assume that there was such an objective need and that the prisoner could be brought to feel the need, whether real or not.

The key element behind the TC is the "latent authority" of the staff. It is symbolized most effectively by the electronically controlled riot door, but more directly by the selection procedure for admission to the TC. The staff has the power to decide who comes into the unit or who is to be removed, to determine the appropriate mix of prisoners, and ulimately has all the power of the prison itself. On the one hand the TC creates relative privileges for a small group who are elected to responsible jobs and carry on the work of the staff among the other prisoners. They fulfill such jobs as chairman or secretary of the meeting in the TC, and this would impress a parole board favourably. On the other hand, in the attempts to mix the prisoners, the decision is not based on choosing only manageable or passive inmates who presumably would be easy to control. Rather a few prisoners with some prestige and authority in the prison (known as "orangutans" by the staff) are also accepted. This reproduces a hierarchy among the prisoners who, to a degree, police themselves. Matters such as stealing are expected to be handl)d by the prisoners. The staff will recount stories of violent reprisals taken by some prisoners against others in response to these alleged internal crimes which express unofficial encouragement for these acts.

It is not clear whether separate incarceration provides the most effective means of social control. The retention of the "mixture" may sacrifice some of the principles of rehabilitation but provide for internal control among the prisoners themselves, not so much in the sense that the inexperienced exercise a moderating effect on the more prison-wary, but that the experienced prisoners pacify the younger, more impulsive and rebellious youngsters through direct explication and demonstration of the limits practically possible in the prison both formally and informally.

The administration is aware of the compromised nature of
the TC, even in this conceptual form. When the prisoner is
outside the TC but within the remainder of the prison he is
subject to the same authority structure as any other inmate.
This reduces the formal potential of his decision-making to the
level of petty regulations associated with getting along with
the other prisoners in his unit. With respect to the question
of decision-making, one prisoner complained that "we have 90
per cent of the say, and no power". The prisoners must fulfil
the normal expectations of prison routine and should they
refrain from going to work could be subject to such punitive
measures as "dissociation". The function of the TC as a means
for management of the prisoners was demonstrated during a
disturbance in Springhill. One living unit broke up its cells,
the prisoners refused to go to work and a disturbance disrupted
the kitchen area. Some prisoners in the TC not only refused to
participate in the incident (thereby, according to the staff,
breaking the inmate code) but volunteered to go and clean up
the cafeteria as well as to serve the food.

When it was first opened the TC was attacked both by some
of the administrators, who resented any degree of prisoner
autonomy--even the appearance of such--and predicted dire consequences, and the excluded prisoners who viewed the TC as a
divisive element which provided another means of differentially
treating prisoners by creating new disparties and distributing
selective rewards. As the TC evolved away from its original
intent and authority was reasserted, the remaining units were
brought into the modified Living Unit scheme which generalized
some of the administrative benefits of the TC to the other
units. According to the administration this has served to
lessen the jealousy of the other prisoners and cut down on the
number of "headaches". It is presented as the application of
the TC principle to the other units, in a modified form suitable to meet the conditions. In fact the therapeutic component
of the philosophy behind the TC was virtually abandoned and any
involvement of the prisoners in the Living Units in the internal order serves the function of increasing staff knowledge
of the state of the units and of enrolling representatives of
the prisoners in compromised situations.

The philosophy of the TC in practice provides for the
appearance of horizontal authority based on the threatened and
actual use of degrees of vertical power to reinforce the limits
imposed on the former. It is still asserted that the degree of
autonomy--and more importantly the therapeutic personal relations and close contact with the staff--are rehabilitative, and
the amount of autonomy granted to prisoners corresponds to the
degree of freedom they can reasonaby handle. This represents
the process of excising the heart of reform in the interests of
maintaining control. The process of control within the TC and,
to a lesser extent in the other units, is a complex one. Many
dedicated professionals and volunteers spend considerable time

and energy assisting prisoners to overcome some of their real
psychological deficits. But in the longer run these have
little to do with criminality in society and in the short run
internal to the prisons, in the crunch, rehabilitation is
sacrificed for control.

The Living Unit Programme

The CPS decided to introduce the Living Unit Program in
all medium security institutions rather than expand the number
of Therapeutic Communities. The spirit of the Living Unit
Program is defined by the CPS as "getting to know, understanding, coupled with interaction between individuals and groups".
Better interpersonal relationships between staff and inmates
would help the inmates acquire social skills necessary for
coping in the community. Communication is now supposed to be
the key concept. The Living Unit is considered a framework
within which each institution can experiment with their own
programme. As a modification of the therapeutic community, the
philosophy emphasises democratic discussion and problem-solving
through group meetings. It was first introduced at Warkworth in
1969 and gradually introduced into other institutions so that
by 1971, the living unit concept was established as the fundamental rehabilitative programme in all medium security institutions, with minimums intended as the next type of institution
to be changed over by 1973. Even maximums were being considered for this change.

Programme development is the responsibility of a psychologist who is assisted by other social specialists. The new
image created is supposed to lessen inmate hostility toward
authority and promote a manageable relationship. The Livng
Unit officer remains in the same living unit during his shift
in order to create a close inmate-staff relationship, which is
expected to result in greater staff involvement helping inmates
"manage their restrictions". In the words of the Canadian
Penitentiary Service, a living unit is like "a home in a vil-
lage". The living unit staff are complemented by security
staff who are seen as equally important and provide constant
surveillance. The Range Officers are replaced at night by
security guards and the cell doors are locked. The real community outside the prison is brought into the Living Unit
Program in the form of community groups and individuals. Some
inmates are also taken out into the community. The CPS views
the Living Unit Programme as the most ambitious it has ever
undertaken, but the Programme has yet to be evaluated.

In the Living Units (LU's) in Springhill there are range
meetings once every two weeks. The functions of these is not
identical with the therapeutic meetings in the TC but evolved
from this idea. Generally, only those issues concerning concrete issues in the management of the range are discussed.
When decisions have to be made as a unit then a representative

is elected from each range who then attends another meeting with staff at which decisions are made. This procedure provides an avenue for prisoner input into the decision-making process, but more importantly for the functioning of the unit, it provides for the communication of official decisions through the prisoners' representatives, thereby attempting to provide some legitimation for the process and involving prisoners in its implementation.

The Range Officers in the LU handle a case load of about six or seven prisoners which provides an opportunity for what is described as personal contact necessary for the handling of individual problems. From this close contact, the Range Officer is usually on top of what is happening in the unit, a point with important implications for control. There are also some chaplains and counselling psychologists, although too few in number to allow for long-term individual counselling. The LU concept was brought to Springhill in October 1972 and was described as similar to the TC with the major distinction being that the cells were locked at eleven p.m. rather than being left open continuously. The direction of change is to erase the distinctions between the two, usually to the detriment of the Therapeutic Community concept.

The staff in the LUs by and large is not composed of professionals, with the exception of some social scientists and clergy. The range officers are largely drawn from the surrounding area and trained on the job, with the officer learning mostly by experience. He is socialized into the norms governing staff behaviour by his superior and other Range Officers and by the prisoners. There is also a weekly one-hour staff meeting with the consulting psychiatrist. The purpose of these general staff meetings has moved away from the type of sensitivity training encouraged earlier and is oriented towards the implementation of policy decisions.

Out of this continued flow of innovation and experimentation in treatment programmes comes the call for more research and planning. The Solicitor General's statement on corrections in 1973 stressed the need for strengthening the co-ordination of corrections. It reported that the development and application of statistical data is badly needed and asked for a closer look at some of the 'innovative' programmes. Were they working? Did they prevent offenders from recidivating? Correctional officials began to think seriously about these questions. By the time the rehabilitation philosophy was receiving concrete implementation in Canada, social processes were developing elsewhere which had already brought the concept into question.

CHAPTER SEVEN

CRITICAL CRIMINOLOGY AND THE NEW REFORMISM

Introduction

The development of a new rehabilitative model of prison reform in the post-1945 decade coincided with the predominance of a structural functional theory in American sociology. The philosophy of rehabilitation was compatible with the consensus framework implied in functional theory. It stressed the legitimate socialization of deviant individuals into the general, law-abiding social norms of the majority, a universal goal of any social structure. The assumption that deviance was pathological reinforced this perspective and justified intervention into the life, attitudes and psyche of the deviant as being in his or her own best interests. Consensus theory did not theorize the existence of any fundamental conflict in the sense that there were groups in society with interests which could not be reconciled. Law was a codified expression of the will and the consciousness of the majority and was ultimately in the best interests of all members of society.

The optimism of this theory was reflected in the growth of the interventionist state in capitalist societies. Both this optimism and the social programmes which were its concrere expression were undergirded by cold war prosperity; both were subsequently undermined by the march of historical events. The most important of these occurred in the United States, but they had some practical consequences and affected ideological developments in Canada. In the middle and late 1960s, with an increasingly unpopular war, with an accompanying mass anti-war movement, with minority group struggles and an approaching economic crisis in the West which was to strike the predominantly Anglo-Saxon countries particularly hard, it became more clear that a consensus model of society was unrealistic. The fact of pervasive, deeply rooted conflict, to which the functionalists had been blinkered, exposed the particular ideological, interest-bound basis of the theory. In this general social turmoil the question of the prison became especially controversial.

The social conflict which erupted in the 1960s formed the backdrop of a radical critique which sought to expose the ideological implications of the consensus thesis. The emergence of "critical criminology" in the 1970s had precedents in the history of criminology, but more fundamentally it was the application of the diverse currents of thought which had resurfaced in academic circles at the time. These ranged from liberal critiques of existing society on such grounds as the lack of equal opportunity on the one hand, to varieties of

Marxism on the other. Even among the latter there was little
uniformity. Epistemologically, they ranged from a near-func-
tional structuralism and economic determinism to the revival of
extreme voluntarism. Critical criminology had a similar
diverse parentage and many currents are reflected in the discipline, with each often having more in common with certain non-
radical forms of theorizing than with many of the newer alternative forms (cf. Cohen 1971:16). While generalizations are
especially difficult to make concerning this body of ideas, one
element in common was the desire to dispose of the corpse of
rehabilitation. The radical theorists argued that, contrary to
the consensus views, there were fundamental discrepancies in
society. Different social groups had different and conflicting
interests, and all were engaged in the struggle for power in
order that their ideas would be represented in law. According
to the proponents of pluralism, law was the outcome of a compromise in which all social groups had influence. In response
to this view, the new radical pluralism asserted that law was
the codification of the interests of one particular social
group, and expressed these interests against those of other
groups.

The conflict perspective undermined the theoretical basis
of rehabilitation, the basis of the liberal stance. If there
was no general social consensus, but only powerful and powerless groups, then the social scientist was forced to grant the
dominant values validity on other grounds, or to reject the
concept of reformation altogether. Consequently most of the
radical criminologists remained marginal to the attempt to
implement reform programmes in prisons, although as we will
indicate, there is a special sense in which critical theorists
have attempted to intervene positively in the social process.
As usual the actual attempt to refurbish the ideal of rehabili-
tation--the new reformism--rested on liberal social theory.
Some liberals, who had demanded that the reforms which had been
devised over the last quarter century should be implemented,
also abandoned the notion that criminality represented a
treatable illness. They advanced instead more sophisticated
theories of objective deficiency, such as the problem of
inherited learning disabilities (cf. Coons 1982), and the
failure of criminals to develop appropriate life skills (cf.
Reher and Neissner 1977). These explanations were still predicted on the assumption that criminals were somehow lacking
something which non-criminals possessed.

Benevolence and Injustice

The prison system has never been without its critics; the
question has always been the theoretical basis and ideological
implications of the criticisms. During the 1950s and early
1960s, while the rehabilitation philosophy was receiving much
attention and some concrete application, the predominant orientation of the critiques involved a debate within a narrow

consensus, which accepted the legitimacy of existing social institutions and focussed on the question of how best to achieve the goal of the reforming prison. Things have noticeably changed in academic circles, and since the middle 1960s there has been a tendency to question the underlying theoretical assumptions of rehabilitation rather than merely the best means to attain the ends (Hawkins 1974:101-102). This does not imply that most criminologists ceased arguing in favour of rehabilitation and disputing appropriate means to this end; rather it is to underscore the significant development of a new orientation adopted by representatives of the latest generation of criminologists who claimed to be critical not only of the implementation of the rehabilitative philosophy but of its ideological foundation. Rehabilitation, it was argued, had totalitarian implications. In the words of Norwal Morris: "The jailer in a white coat and wih a doctorate remains a jailer-- but with larger powers over his fellows". The totalitarian implications of rehabilitation had violated the human rights of the inmates: "our benevolence", he wrote, had been "untrammelled by any sense of injustice" (1972:472).

The intellectual basis of the change in criminological theory can be found in the apparent failure of programmes to rehabilitate. Numerous studies indicated that the programmes themselves, despite varied content, different locations and separate times, were not as successful as had been anticipated. The general conclusion was drawn that, despite a few positive indications, the type of programme which prisoners underwent did not have a significant effect on the outcome. The rate of recidivism was generally no better than expected for any group of prisoners and those programmes with relatively high levels of success tended to choose prisoners with a higher probability of not being re-convicted (Bottoms and McClintock 1973; England 1955; Hood and Spark 1970; Bailey 1966; Grant 1960; Clinard 1968; Vold 1954; Hood 1971; Lipton, Martinson and Wilkes 1975).

Since most convicts had connections in varying degrees with the "street" it was suggested that they entered prison with sub-cultural values which tended to militate against reform (Irwin and Cressey 1962; Cline 1969). Furthermore, operating parallel to and undermining the treatment programme, the process of re-socialization within the prison shaped attitudes and behaviours which were assumed to be inimical to the achievement of the treatment goals (Garabedian 1963). Anti-administrative behaviour (defined as "anti-social" by penologists) was rewarded in the prison "culture" in which the successful circumvention of prison rules enhanced prestige among prisoners (Schrag 1971).

The treatment process did not operate in a vacuum but on the contrary competed with other influences which were seen by many prisoners as more important and which tended to undercut the potential effectiveness of programmes. When prisoners did

participate in a programme, they usually defined it as a necessary short-term compromise, or as a learned response to a
coercive situation. But it had no significance beyond the
context of the prison and therefore was ultimately of no rehabilitative value.

A prisoners' probability of success, generally defined as
not being reconvicted after release, has frequently been found
to be more important than the characteristics of any specific
rehabilitation programme (England 1955). Studies have identified some factors in a prisoner's background which are associated with the potential for "going straight" such as social
class, education, prior delinquincy, employment experience,
drug use, criminal record, type of offense, and so on (Glaser
1964; Wilkins 1969). Prior selection of programme participants
then, may significantly shape the ultimate outcome and the type
of treatment may have little significant independent effect.

Evaluations which find negative correlations between
treatment and success are much less frequently reported than
those which report findings of a positive direction (Bailey
1966; cf. Haley and Lerette 1983:36-39). One study in the
field of addiction, however, found a negative correlation between success of treatment (defined as the percentage of
prisoners "quite certain" or "reasonably certain" to be drug
free) and the number of periods of clinical treatment (Beech
and Gregerson 1964), the more time spent in the treatment
clinic the less likely were the participants to be free of
drugs after release. It was concluded that the experimental
programme had inadvertently promoted more successful criminals
(Murphy 1970). Findings such as this have the effect of sensi-
tizing the researcher to the social meaning of the programme
external to the premises upon which it is undertaken.

The response to these findings varied among criminologists. The strict conservative response was largely a reiteration of the goal of punishment and the rejection of both the
philosophy of rehabilitation as well as the possibility of
reformation. The findings of the critics could be used as
ammunition against any attempt, either individual or institutional, at reform in the prison. At the opposite end of the
scale, the more or less radical responses similarly rejected
rehabilitation and reformation, not disputing their possibility
but rather their absolute necessity or desirability. These
reactions were to be expected. The philosophy of rehabilitation, however, was tied most closely with liberal criminology.

The Prison: A Monumental Mistake

The liberal criminologists reacted to the failure of
rehabilitation in a number of ways. Some continued to accept
the philosophy as it had been enunciated and took the position
that what was widely regarded as its failure was, on the con-

trary, the failure to implement the ideal correctly. It was a matter of insufficient resources, an inadequate number of staff, or a lack of motivation. As David Stang (1974) expressed this viewpoint: "there is no reason other than lack of...will why rehabilitation and incarceration must continue to be two mutually exclusive goals". His programme suggestions amount to a reorganization of the vocational and academic training facilities which, while useful as far as they go, do not address the question of the failure to rehabilitate. From being a popular mode to actually deepen the punishment of imprisoned people, the tread-mill became a common image to represent the futility of prison reform. Even the greater energy put into programmes had all come to nought because of the overwhelming magnitude of the negative force that was the prison.

Thomas Murton, himself a liberal reformer, described this process from the inside. He distinguished between a "real reformer" who entered the realm of prison administration following a critical period with notions of restructuring it, and what he termed the "official reformer" (1976). Various reform proposals would be suggested by the real liberal reformer which would have a progressive character. However he would not be granted an opportunity to implement his projects fully, "because the free society does not really want reform but merely an abatement of brutality and inhuman conditions" (:163-165). At a certain point an "official reformer" is appointed and the content of the reform proposal is undermined. Prison reforms, then, are cyclical in nature, and the end of the process is to end up virtually in the same position prior to the intervention of the "real reform"; the prison usually returns to the status quo ante. Although this may accurately describe the process, the failure of reform should be explained more directly by discussing the role of intervening causes rather than generalizing about the putative wishes of society as a whole.

A second response rejected the concept of rehabilitation while maintaining the necessity of incarcerating those defined as criminals. In Britain, Sir Rupert Cross (1971) questioned less the means to achieve rehabilitation, and more the goal itself. Cross's work is a denunciation of the medical model in criminology, and a critique of the prison as a "cold storage depot". He is sceptical about the extent to which rehabilitation is achievable by educational and vocational training, declares "deterioration" in the prison to be as likely as reform and argues that real individual reformation occurs only in the most exceptional cases. The myth of rehabilitation produced only more suffering as prison sentences were lengthened to allow time for the supposed changes in personality to take place. Consequently, prison sentences should be shortened to meet only the ends aready legitimately set: denunciation, deterrence, and the protection of the public (Hawkins 1974: 103-104; Bean 1976).

For Cross, then, prisons are appropriate institutions but the view that people can be reformed in them is a myth. His argument implies the need for a better classification system to specify those who are criminogenic while keeping the rest out of prison as much as possible. For the majority, the process of reformation is unproblematic because they are essentially like us; for the minority of incorrigibles, reformation is unworkable in principle. In this view the liberal and conservative arguments merge in a new synthesis. Cross retains the conservative view of prison as a place of confinement and punishment and rejects the theory of rehabilitation which held that individual reformation was possible in the prison. At the same time he modified the dichotomy between the criminal and the non-criminal by narrowing the definition of the former while at the same time accepting that they were in principle unchangeable.

The acknowledgement that the prison system had failed to reform those in its custody had led liberal criminologists to the point of abandoning the prison as a viable reformative strategy. Attempts to develop institutional structures embodying the medical model--in particular the concept of the "therapeutic prison"--were declared to be unworkable. This entailed abandoning the philosophy of rehabilitation based on the medical model, although not the goal of reformation. Robert Martinson, one of the most widely quoted critics of the rehabilitation model (cf. 1979), called for most prisons to be "gradually torn down". However, there was need for "remaining facilities", small and presumably humane prisons, for those considered dangerous to society. But, he concludes, "let us give up the comforting myth" that prisons "can be changed into hospitals" (Martinson 1972; cf. Parizeau and Szabo 1977; Kirkpatrick and McGrath 1976).

Not all, or even most, criminologists were content with dismissing the prison as an instrument of reform. The main point of these criticisms which was new was that the type of rehabilitation programmes did not make a significant difference. This did not necessarily mean to some penologists that other programmmes, instituted within a prison or involving some liason with the community, might not be successful (cf. Ross and MacKay 1978; Jackson 1981). In this view the goal of rehabilitation was reaffirmed although some aspects of the philosophy were necessarilly abandoned. The view that it was still possible to reform prisoners led to the development of modified versions of the medical model of corrections. Gill, for example, declared that the "progressive prison" (as distinct from the "custodial prison" which had dominated prior to the adoption of rehabilitation) had failed. A prison is not, he asserted, a composite clinic, school, factory, and social club. These have nothing to do with the fundamental reason for failure, which is criminality itself. In his call for a "professional prison" for the "tractable" prisoner (1972:115-116), he argued that the reformable majority could be treated in prisons, by specialists with professional training in rehabilitation. He maintains the dichotomy and the view that the appropriate reformative agency is a body of experts institutionalized for that purpose.

The Social Context of the Prison Community

Within liberal criminology the studies of the social structure of the prison were also re-evaluated as part of the general trend to widen the horizons and consider some of the implications of the society of which the prison was a part. While criticizing early organizational sociologists for failing to situate the prison contextually and regarding it as an autonomous institution, the relationship between the prison and the society was still handled within the ideological framework of trying to understand individual criminality.

Although he was critical of the functionalist tendency to study the prison in isolation, Wheeler's concern continued to be the functioning of the inmate system (1971). He singled out two explanations of the inmate culture. The first, social anthropological in origin, argued that prisoners bring with them into the prison criminogenic attitudes which reject "conventional norms and values". Since prisons contain a majority of people who embody criminalistic values, these values would predictably be reinforced and generalized to those less engrained. Prisonization, then, tends to deepen in degree as imprisonment continues (Schrag 1971) but the source of the prison culture, the place where the ideals originate, is in the society as a whole, outside the prison.

Alternatively, Sykes and Messinger (1971) argued that the development of a prison culture was more a response to the conditions of deprivation within the prison. This theory explained the normative order and the differentiation of the roles of the prisoners as distinct responses to the deprivations. The process of adopting the values of the inmate culture was not linear; the prisoners did not simply become more anti-administrative in their values as time went on. Rather the point of time they were generally most opposed to the prison regime was around the middle of their sentence. As the end of their period of confinement approached, and the possibility of parole loomed, the prisoners modified some of their prison-determined values and tended to revert to their previous behaviours. Prisonization, then, was better represented by a "U-shaped" curve with the middle point of the curve indicating the time during the sentence with the greatest degree of departure from the values of the prison administration and, supposedly, society as a whole.

In order to determine to what extent the solidary inmate

code resulted from the conditions of the prison or rather
reflected values developed outside the prison, Wheeler adopted
a cross-cultural perspective and examined prisons in Scandinavia. His study indicated that a prison with significant deprivations need not generate inmate solidarity, and he concluded
that deprivations themselves were not sufficient "for the emergence of a strong and resistive inmate value system" (Wheeler
1971:104). His conclusion goes beyond the characteristics of
the prison itself and argues that the crucial component in
determining how prisoners respond to imprisonment is the
characteristics of their nation or community. In Scandinavia
the general lower level of violence and the lack of a "we-they"
perspective "would seem to reflect the relatively narrow range
of the stratification system, the virtual absence of American-
style slums, and the greater homogeneity of...society", as well
as the individualistic, isolated outlook thought to be characteristic of Scandinavian peoples (:106). He found that the
extent to which prisoners were socially deprived, that is, the
degree of enforced isolation, was inversely related to opposition towards the staff. The more the prisoners were isolated
from each other the lower the degree of anti-staff feelings
(:112). It is difficult to imagine what kind of "inmate culture" could be formed by isolated prisoners. Prisons culture
is a social phenomenon, a collective response to conditions,
and requires a degree of social contact in which attitudes to
the conditions of deprivation can be consciously shared and in
which a collective response can be reinforced.

The importance of this study arises, in part from the view
that prison need not, by virtue of the characteristic deprivations of the systems, lead by some general social rule to an
institutionalized hostility which results in some degree of
inmate solidarity against the staff. However, social conditions in American history (and the social character of American
prisons) make the development of this perspective probable on
the part of many disadvantaged individuals.

Evidence is further provided that prisons with "a fairly
rich and complex set of treatment goals and programmes" demonstrate less solidarity opposition on the part of inmates
(:112). This highlights the recognition that institutional
structures can be developed for purposes of sub-cultural management in the prison. But the studies are restricted to those
institutions with a "rich" programme, that is, in which the
development of positive alternatives in corrections has supplemented the strictly punitive orientation. The point is to
recognize the central function of the treatment staff in the
maintenance of social control in those institutions where such
intervention is likely to be successful, if not in rehabilitating, then in controlling. The conclusions drawn about the
failure of rehabilitation address only the putative goal of
individual reformation but do not question the role played by
the "jailors in white coats" in minimizing internal control

problems. This is a double-edged sword, as indicated by the
hostility that frequently exists between the guards and the
treatment staff. The point is that reforms are contradictory
in nature: they can pacify the target population, especially
when implemented from above. But they can also create conditions which are conducive to the development of new demands, a
potential which underscores the possibilities of progressive
collective action. The failure of rehabilitation became significant when it ceased to play a pacifying role in the prison;
its social control aspect was paramount for the prison administration.

The studies selected for review by Wheeler which take the
"external world" into consideration still have their focus on
the characteristics of inmates which are associated with the
social roles they play in prison--in particular with those who
adopt anti-staff attitudes. Since "inmate life generally reflects broader cultural conditions" (:112) then it becomes more
difficult to restructure the prison to eliminate the internal
social system.

In his critique of the organizational sociologists,
Wheeler is concerned with the relationship between the prison
and the outside world not with regard to the function of the
prison as an institution, but with a concern for the effects of
the characteristics of individual prisoners arising from their
outside experiences on the social control in the prison. In
the end, Wheeler acknowledges the new 1960s orthodoxy by de-
claring that more staff or better programmes would make little
difference, and that a much more radical reorientation of
prison organizations is necessary in order to produce a prison
that would make a difference. What was required was something
innovative to achieve the same goals. During the 1970s a new
current of treatment programmes emphasizing the importance of
the community context was implemented in Canada and elsewhere.
An analysis of some attempts to develop programmes incorpora-
ting the new reformism will be presented below. Within North
America, however, the question of criminal justice as a whole
was increasingly questioned by radical scholars.

Critical Theory

The undermining of the rehabilitative model of corrections
had as its upshot the development of a new "critical criminology". While sometimes basing itself on fairly well established traditions of middle class radicalism, the new criminology adopted perspectives which were different from those
dominant in official circles, whether conservative or liberal.

In contrast to the changes in liberal views, which became
the basis of the new reformism, one tendency within critical
theory remained mostly academic and offered few if any direct
programmatic implications which could be adopted by the reform-

ers. In principle standing apart from the social process to avoid contamination, the social scientists could offer an intellectual critique which, in some ways, was more accurate because less connected with the particular interests associated with prison and prison reform. The argument is that the liberal reformers often have an interest in maintaining the prison reforms, and thence the prison, although they may become more cynical about their effectiveness. Critical theorists only have an interest in that social structure which will provide a forum for their views and reward them suitably according to merit. The critic, then, can come the closest to exposing the interests behind the liberal theory and programme, while eschewing the task of helping to develop an alternative.

Perhaps the fundamental argument used to undermine one of the pillars of the classical law and order approach was the argument that the distinction which is drawn between criminals and non-criminals, and the resulting conception that the object of reformation is to transform the former into the latter, was mistaken. This argument was supported by data from self-report studies which appeared to show that the vast majority of the population had, at one time or another, acted in an illegal way for which, if apprehended, they could have been subject to legal sanctions (Radzinowicz 1964; Hood and Spark 1970; Turk 1969). Criminality, then, was pervasive and any research which was confined to a study of those in penal institutions was biased if they were regarded as representative of "criminals" distinct from the remainder of the population. Empirically there was some significant differences between those in and out of jails, but this was explained with reference to other social factors--in particular social class and race--which made them, for socially determinable reasons, more subject to conviction. But there were no significant differences between "criminals" and "non-criminals"; by and large this was a false distinction. While not denying that those defined as criminals were unrepresentative of the social spectrum, the radical approaches asserted that this fact had less to do with the character of criminals but rather reflected either differential access to legal counsel or a socially acquired acquiescence to a situation of unequal power.

As new legislation extends the realm of potentially criminal social action, the focus in criminology became centered on the criminal justice system itself rather than on the criminal (Quinney 1975; cf. Schwendinger and Schwendinger 1975). Studies demonstrated that judges sentenced criminals and parole boards released prisoners not on the sole basis of scientific principles but rather according to more particularistic criteria. The most severe negative sanctions were applied systematically against "losers": those in casual labour, on welfare, in mental institutions in ghettos and slums who had not been successful because of racism, class discrimination and so on. This was the universe from which most "criminals" were drawn, leading to the conclusion that crime could not be dealt with as a separate problem, but rather: "In the long run...our hope for the prevention of crime must depend on the inroads we can make on the structure of contemporary poverty (Conrad 1974: 205; cf. Becker 1968).

This position ignores the pervasiveness of criminal activity among the population, and does not suggest that there are criminals--even within the standard definition but more so according to the wider and more radical definitions--among the winners (cf. Downes and Rock 1979). But in seeing criminality as a response of the powerless to concrete social conditions, the "problems" perspective opens up the possibility of restructuring social relationships in some fashion, and provides a basis for social theory which could deduce appropriate action. Furthermore, to focus on those who, above all, are deemed to be criminal and have sanctions imposed on them, is necessary in order to understand the function of law as an instrument of control in the hands of powerful groups (cf. Tepperman 1977).

Within the radical framework, an economic theory of crime was associated with direct environmental causation. To the extent that individuals were subject to social and psychological deficits, these inequalities could be the breeding ground for many behaviours which contravened legal statutes. McDonald, however, has disconfirmed the direct link between social problems and crime--with the exception of unemployment (1976: 154-155; cf. Fattah 1983). This is consistent with a second hypothesis associated with critical theory which links general affluence with an increasing crime rate. Crime is socially constructed and varies with the resources of social control. The liberal solution to law and order--more police, schools, reformatories--contribute to this construction (Reasons 1977:411). Similarly, it has been argued that recessions can logically lead to less criminality. As life styles are adversely affected, a "survival ethic" surfaces emphasizing family values and engendering a conservative attitude towards property crime (cf. Wright 1981). Economically difficult circumstances, then, can be associated in theory with both a potential for criminal activity and for a law-and-order philosophy.

The Prison as Liberal-Totalitarian

How people were unequally charged and sentenced were major issues in this critique of the system of justice. With respect to the prison, the liberal-radical critique of rehabilitation usually rests in part on the view that in practice the activities of the prison regime are authoritarian in content and socialize individuals to function in an anti-democratic setting. The experiences in prison are therefore "dysfunctional to democracy" (Murton 1976: 73-74). The individual conforms to the rules and regulations to avoid punishment or curry favour within a coercive situation. Wright argues that the prison trains for social conformity rather than democracy which is synonymous with political activism. The prison is attempting, in a totalitarian fashion, to diminish disrespect for authority and make prisoners into strict conformists to coercive agents and rules (Murton: 166; Wright 1976: 152-157).

The prison, according to Wright, is "liberal-totalitarian" in form, the liberalism implying the philosophy of rehabilitation and the totalitarianism meaning the attempt to induce strict conformity to authority. He argues that, on the one hand, liberal means are used to further totalitarian ends. The liberal programmes implemented become devices for furthering the values of the prison: obedience and compliance to authoritarian rule. In practice they become the antithesis of the reform philosophy in which terms they were implemented. And "totalitarian means"--the fact of imprisonment itself with all that entails--are expected to produce liberal ends (cf. Quinney 1970: 178). The aim of rehabilitation is to alter certain attitudes of certain prisoners, especially "to destroy the rebellious spirit of prisoners, to break them into conformity" (Wright 1976: 325). While most prisoners only potentially adopt this solidary opposition model, the authorities conclude that such prisoners are most in need of rehabilitation, and must stay longer in prison. If seen as incorrigible in their attitude of rebellion, they become candidates for the next super-maximums planned in the future.

In Wright's approach, activity defined as criminal is inherently rational. This view rejects any notion that the offender is psychologically sick and therefore in need of treatment, an approach which degrades the prisoner and leads ultimately to the conversion of prisons into "mental hospitals". The treatment philosophy emerges as a major legitimation with which to justify attempts to control the disadvantaged. It is doubtful whether apparently "irrational" crimes, however, can simply be ignored or attributed to the tendency of the media to sensationalize. To recognize that the social structure engenders forms of psychological debilitation is to endorse the need for some form of individual reformation, which Wright is unwilling to do. Ultimately, theory must account for both structural and "irrational" crime and take seriously the need for individual rehabilitation while eschewing the belief that it can have any long-term significance for individuals in the absence of a change in theirt social circumstances, or for society as a whole in the absence of a progressive movement for social change.

The strength of Wright's analysis of rational crime rests on one key element of this need for reformation. If there is nothing wrong with criminals except a lack of opportunity to solve socially created problems, then the suppression of people defined as criminals is merely a response which blames indi-

viduals for social inequalities. Criminality becomes, in this
view, an implicit indictment of the social order. The use of
social control can only be justified if the development of
society is such as to progressively and fundamentally eliminate
these social inequalities. The failure of Western nations to
achieve a major redistribution of wealth during this century is
an indictment which exposes the ideological content of law and
order rhetoric and undermines the justification of punishment.

Labeling: The Radical Version

     A further development in the recognition of the negative
effects of being processed by the criminal justice system had
its origins in social interactionist theory. Long before the
development of radical criminoloy, it had been recognized that
the stigma attached to the term "criminal" had social consequences for the labeled individual irrespective of whether the
label had been correctly applied, that is, according to the
prevailing code. Such a process had the effect of reinforcing
those traits which were endemic to the definition. In its
earlier version this view assumed that the label effectively
exaggerated what was already present (Becker 1963).

     Subsequently with the growth of phenomenology and its
application to sociology, the act of labeling was regarded as
the basis of deviance: deviance was engendered by the terms
used to decribe it, a view earlier posited by Tannenbaum (1938;
cf. Taylor, Walton and Young 1973: 141). It was the action
taken with respect to the performance of a certain act which
imposed the "criminal" label on individuals, rather than the
performance of certain acts. The absolutist extension of this
perspective suggests that crime would not exist as a phenomenon
if no one was ever defined as a "criminal". For more practical
purposes, the labeling (or interactionist) approach focuses on
one particular important effect, the societal reaction to
crime, and rejects the more extreme implications which follow
when the phenomenological approach is taken to its logical
conclusion (Wheeler and Cottrell, 1969; cf. Ericson 1975; Schur
1971).

     Labeling theory has been associated with liberal (Lemert
1967) as well as conservative implications (Gouldner 1968).
The labeling perspective, however, had radical implications as
well. Since social groups were unequal in power, the dominant
group would be in a position to determine those actions which
were to be defined legally as criminal. A distinct radical or
"critical" version emerged, based partly on this understanding,
and partly on a critique of labeling theory, especially when it
was inflated to the status of a full theory of deviance. Critical theory claimed that by accepting the definitions of
criminality current in society, the liberal theorists, at the
least, were accepting implicitly the values of the dominant
group while proclaiming value neutrality. In contrast, the

radical criminologists rejected the philosophical claims for a value-free science and openly proclaimed support for the powerless. Critical theory claimed that there was nothing inherently deviant about any behaviour--deviance was socially defined. Any notion of a social consensus was rejected and it was claimed that deviant definitions were imposed by those in superordinate positions with the power to create such definitions. Hence it was merely a case of powerful individuals or groups defining as criminal those deviant acts of other individuals or groups which in some way infringed upon their own dominant position. Therefore, they concluded, crime had no ontological reality--it did not really exist--but was simply a social definition in principle subject to change with a change of the dominant group. To agree that certain actions were criminal meant accepting the dominant definitions and therefore being on the side of the powerful. The only way to be on the side of the powerless was to assert that crimes did not exist, that they were merely dominant group fictions. The jump was made from the assertion that what is defined as a crime is relative to the specific social structure, to the absolutist position that, therefore, crimes do not exist.

The value-engaged labeling approach opens up the possibility of questioning why certain acts are labeled as criminal while others are not, but it begs the question whether, in principle, certain actions of a socially defined nature ought to be disapproved and subject to some form of social sanction. Its progressive side questions the genesis of criminal definitions, and could lead to the concrete examination of the social structure in order to understand how specific social groups use legal definitions to protect their position from other groups with whom they have contradictory interests. The negation of the consensus framework opens up the possibility of a systematic social critique. It becomes possible to ask why some actions are criminal while others are not and to question the basis on which criminal laws are made.

The Social Construction of Criminological Theory

This crucial issue of the genesis of criminal law and criminal definitions is central to critical criminology. As we have argued above, this ideological development has a number of diverse currents. Recently some promising developments have occurred in the application of a political economy model to Canadian corrections (cf. Ratner 1984). Our concern here is with one of the two principal exaggerations of such a model: the over-emphasis on social action found in voluntaristic forms of theorizing. Although perhaps the most significant of these developments have occurred in the adoption of an interactionist labeling perspective, within a self-defined Marxist criminology the most revealing attempt to develop a phenomenological basis for "critical criminology" can be found in the early work of Richard Quinney. In 1970 he proposed the development of a theoretical perspective which would "provide a reorientation to the study of crime" (1970: v; cf. Taylor, Walton and Young 1973).

Quinney's theory of crime begins with the assumption, common to much critical theory, that power is the most basic characteristic of any social structure. The analysis begins with the discrepancy between those with and those without power. Conflict, which is produced by this unequal distribution, is essentially competition for power and is endemic to all societies. Social stability is ensured primarily by coercion and constraint rather than consensus. Coercion is not only physical, Quinney argues, because "institutional means are used to officially establish and enforce sets of values for the entire population" (1970: 11). It is not surprising, then, that empirical studies discover there to be a certain level of agreement in the population concerning the types of criminal acts which deserve punishment. Contrary to the belief of some liberal sociologists , this finding does not constitute a refutation of critical theory.

While the conflict perspective is regarded by Quinney as an appropriate model for power relationships within the society as a whole, the social struture is composed of numerous interest groups internal to which the consensus model applies (:9). One of these groups will hold the position of paramount power in society, and it will use this position to protect itself. In particular, it will declare illegal those values and actions of subordinate groups whose interests are most in conflict with its own. Legal policies and penal sanctions are merely definitions applied by the powerful to certain actions of the powerless which threaten their position. Crime, then, is socially constructed and legal definitions are primarily employed to protect the power of the dominant group and secure its interests.

Society consists of a number of "segments" which are "broad statistical aggregates containing persons of similar age, sex, class, status, occupation, race, ethnicity, religion, or the like". An interest is not necessarily an aggregate of all of these characteristics, but one or any combination of them (1970: 39). Segments have objective interests in common which they may or may not recognize. When a segment organizes to achieve its aims it becomes an "interest group". It follows that an individual could belong to any number of segments and interest groups. It is not the discrepancies in "interests" which is the basis of conflict between interest groups, however, but rather "power" itself produces conflict since each group competes for influence to shape public policy. Quinney's pluralism asserts that the various interest groups are "grossly unequal in power". The "public policy", then, is not the outcome of a power struggle between equal and competing agents, but is dominated by the most powerful interests.

The public policy of government (including the laws) is either the result of the power of a dominant interest group (the private government behind the public) or is the government itself organized as a separate interest group. If, in the beginning, the state attempts to act merely as a regulator of the various interest groups, it gradually comes to develop an interest of its own, distinct from the other private groups. But as an interest group which monopolizes power, the state will in the end become another oppressive interest. That is, it will begin by bowing to the "commonweal" but in the end consolidate itself as a distinct interest.

A theoretical problem emerges here, concerning the definition of the commonweal, the common interest. It is not possible to balance the separate interests when the crucial aspect is the competition for power, theorized as an absolute antagonism brooking no final compromise. To the extent that any interest group consolidates, it defines as criminal those actions of interest groups opposed to it, and puts into play institutional mechanisms to diffuse the definition. The absolute antagonism founded on the struggle for power makes the concept of a "commonweal" unthinkable.

Contrary, it would seem, to any possibility consistent with conflict theory, Quinney asserts that the solution to this dilemma is that law must be made "neutral"; it must "necessarily be removed from the control of either the interests of private groups or public government (1970:42). He claims that the present government can still be seen to a degree as a neutral instrument upon which competing interest groups maintain pressure in order to establish the public policy in the interests of the community as a whole. Government (and therefore law) represents the best compromise between competing interest groups. His radical theory at this stage of its development begins to look like the old pluralist theory in new clothes.

If the crucial question is competition for power then it follows that it is in this arena that criminal definitions will most likely be created. Those groups with the greatest amount of power underneath the ruling group itself might possess the greatest threat in the competition for power and therefore ought to be most liable to have their values and actions defined as criminal. This does not happen for it is the formally powerless who most frequently are labelled criminals.

Rather than isolating power from the question of what power is used to do, the question has to come back to the basis of the differences between the competing interest groups. Power is chiefly the result rather than the ultimate basis of the distinction between groups. To understand social conflict we have to examine the social basis of the groups in competition--the struggle for "power" is only an expression of the antagonism between certain groups. This antagonism has an objective basis in the social structure from which conflict springs, connected to, but conceptually distinct from the official organs of power. The wielders of power do so in accordance with their objective position within a determinate social structure. Quinney has presented us with a description but hardly a "theory".

One of the difficulties with this approach arises from the philosophical basis which underlies it. To approach the question of criminality from an alternative theory, beginning with structural processes in society which generate contradictory interests which, in turn, shape the contours of conflict in the society, including the struggle for power, it is necessary to recognize the existence of a "real" world. For Quinney, on the other hand, there are merely "our own subjective, multiple social worlds."(1970: 34) Concepts are not the end result of a process of preception, however modified by experience, based on an objective reality, but are mental constructions. Since there wll be as many mental constructions as there are minds to perceive, then the question arises how to assess which construction is "best". Quinney's concern is the connection between "observation and the utility of such observations in understanding our own subjective multiple worlds" (:4), and he must address the question: on what basis is this utility determined? He begins by rejecting a number of alternative philosophical approaches, the first of these being positivism. Positivism asserted that there was a close connection between what is perceived and what really exists and that, while not able to grasp reality absolutely, the process of the scientific method was a means by which generalizations about objective processes (not necessarily static ones, nor ones that are not affected by both the process of investigation and the application of knowledge) could be developed. In contrast to this, a new "humanist" perspective has been developed which rejects the possibility of social science altogether and thereby undermines the process by which relatively progressive action may be determined. The critique of positivism as being naive in epistemology does not adequately address more sophisticated versions nor, more importantly, other approaches which have developed their own critique of positivist methods.

The basis of the rejection of positivism is a realization that conservative and liberal criminology had implicitly, and frequently explicitly, been supportive of the status quo, that is, of the dominant social group. This critique however, fails to separate the wheat from the chaff. It lumps together separate attributes: positivism maintains a metaphysical separation between the knower and the known; it supposes order to exist independently and hence believes in objective causation; it can only deal in conditions that are given and therefore of necessity supports the status quo, despite its proclamation of value neutrality, and so on (Quinney 1973:2-4). The problems with positivism are assured to be equally based on their uncritical transposition of the natural science model to the study of social phenomena, and the inherent impossibility of the application of the scientific method itself to such phenomena. A science of society is declared to be impossible, and materialism, as the foundation of social science, is discarded. Consequently, when Quinney turns to competing theories of society he begins by asserting: "Social constructionist thought begins with a recognition of philosophical idealism" (1973:5).

Quinney argues that ethnomethodology, a recent outlook which begins and ends with actors' perceptions, sticks too close to a "mentally constructed" reality by focussing only on the images normally developed by social actors in society. It fails "to provide a yardstick for judging the goodness of one reality over another" (1973:7). He declares labelling theory to be progressive because of its libertarian critique of the control of some individuals by others. But social constructionism as a whole does not offer an "image of an authentic existence"; hence it cannot transcend the existing order. It can show what is wrong but cannot present a picture of how things should be.

Phenomenology, for Quinney, comes much closer to fulfilling his criteria of an adequate theory. Essentially he argues that, rather than studying merely things which exist and can be apprehended, the mind can grasp, idealistically, the essence of things. This philosophy allows us to go beyond the present through a process of understanding which arises from comparisons with possible experiences. This conceptualization is crucial to the creation of concepts of a "new existence"; but, argues Quinney, it still does not lead to the overthrowing of the oppressive reality (1973:8-10).

The final step is to criticize what exists by comparing it with what can be imagined; that is, to develop "radical criticism". Essentially this involves liberating yourself from the false consciousness dominant in society, and then through the realm of ideas, transform the consciousness of others. An intellectual movement, a consciousness raising process, is then set in motion which has its expression in an "active life in which we transcend the established existence". In short, for Quinney, there is no reality apart from our consciousness; consciousness creates reality; therefore, a new consciousness can create a new reality.

By negating social science in general, Quinney rejects all versions of an important instrument by which society can be potentialy apprehended in thought as a basis for change. His "liberation" is only a personal one, well within the liberal tradition. It is a purely intellectual exercise by which one reasons through the various competing ideologies and selects the preferred one, the one with the best "ideal" of existence.

When we ask how to achieve this ideal form of life, Quinney can only assert that its diffusion through society as an intellectual movement will have the effect of changing society. His rejection of social science as "positivism" has led him back to the pre-modern Enlightenment which, if it was progressive in its time, is hardly so in the present.

Critiques of critical criminology have usually stressed that the assertion that "modern law in its entirety is a tool by which a handful of powerful persons manage to oppress the rest of us" is oversimplified (Gibbons and Garabedian 1974). Firstly there exists some social consensus regarding the punishment of acts defined as crimes, and secondly rather than oppress us some laws serve to protect us. The first objection misses the point that social definitions, while developed by dominant groups, are diffused throughout society. A social constructionist, for example, would argue that those with differential resources can imprint their ideologies, to a greater or lesser extent depending on objective conditions, on the population as a whole. This ideological hegemony would be likely to produce any consensus that exists. It is also true that deviant perspectives are more likely to be found in specific sub-groups whose objective position increases the probability that they would adopt ideas contrary or at least distinct from those in dominant positions.

The second objection is more serious; but here the problem with critical theory is too great an emphasis on the coercive aspects of social control and not enough attention to the other strategies. Reformism is precisely such a strategy. Specific reforms are insituted that often have their raison d'etre in social action arising from the disadvantaged, but the goals of this action are appropriated by the official representatives and only those aims which are compatible with existing institutions are implemented from the top down. Such laws operate in the interests of the dominant group no less--and frequently more so--than coercive laws, providing that the social structure is able to absorb the changes. In times when this is possible institutions are developed to create "changes" thereby embedding reformism in the social fabric. To the extent that social conflict theory ignores the interaction of the strategies for control, it becomes one-sided and open to the critique of inadequately comprehending the social process.

Too close a connection should not be drawn between consensus theories and policies of repression. Unquestionably, when compared with conflict theories, which tend to be critical of the status quo, consensus theorists tend to sanction repression. This, of course, rests on the belief that the social consensus is really only the position of the "silent majority" and that it is necessary to protect it. But the fundamental question is not repression, per se, but repression as one means of social control, and those in dominant positions have at

their disposal peaceful and reformative options as well. The
use of any given option is tactical and depends on the circumstances. We have argued that the rehabilitative philosophy was
also connected logically with the dominance of consensus
theory. This reformist aspect of control, with alternative
strategies, is frequently not stressed in critical theory which
has been held to assert that "the holders of power...have the
most to gain by a high level of sanctions and a low level of
civil liberties" (McDonald 1975:238). In fact the opposite is
the case in most circumstances. The stability of the social
order is in fact enhanced during periods when reformist options
are available, by the judicious employment of civil liberties.
The extent to which critical theory is tolerated is itself a
measure of the security of the dominant group. As an ideology
of permanent opposition, critical theory is the conscience of
liberalism and in fact flourishes best in a liberal milieux.
The irony is that "critical criticism" attacks the type of
society in which it can best flourish.

Considering its avowed objective as being "value-engaged",
phenomenological critical theory fails to provide any evaluative basis for social action since ultimately this kind of
theory accepts the abyss between the powerful and the powerless
as a universal feature of all societies at all times.

Libertarianism and the Prison

The appeal of idealistic criminology is its moral indictment of unjust social conditions. This critique is at its most
powerful when dissecting the conditions of imprisonment. The
critique of the prison as an instrument of dehumanization is
very powerful. When these oppressive conditions are connected
to a theory of libertarianism, however, the potential for real
social change is actually diminished. Libertarian theorists
reject any concern with social constraints and with the potential need for coercion in social organization.

An expanding and important literature testifies to the
obvious facts of degradation and dehumanization which are the
common fare of life in the prison. It is this kind of impas-
sioned understanding of what the prison actually does to
people--prisoners, guards, immediate families, the public in
general--which underlies the liberal and radical critique of
the prison. Prisons, in this critique, emerge as medieval
fortresses which trap men into a life of crime. "The criminal
is sequestered with other criminals, in conditions exacerbating
the lowest drives of lonely and stranded men, men deprived of
loved ones, of dignifying work, of pacifying amenities...They
are nagged at by petty indignities like having to get along on
one roll of toilet paper per month." (Wills 1975; cf. Schroeder
1976; Caron 1979; American Friends Service Committee 1971).

The libertarian response is for an end to all prisons

immediately. The progressive nature of this kind of literary work is that it exposes conditions in the prisons and undermines the conservative view that prisons are "too soft". But the question has to be asked whether the movement to de-prison society, in its libertarian form, is linked to an adequate social theory. The libertarian view is based on the most extreme form of individualism and has long intellectual roots in personal rebellion back at least to the enlightenment. While in general reflecting a literary and artistic response which negated standard social conventions, libertarian ideals have spread to intellectuals among the middle class.

In the extreme liberal view the individual is counterposed to the social system which is by definition repressive and limiting. The philosophy has been articulated by Robert Pirzig's in his book, Zen and the Art of Motorcycle Maintenance: "He felt that institutions of every sort all tended to direct thought for ends other than truth, for the perpetuation of their own functions and for the control of individuals in the service of these functions." It is a thesis of permanent opposition in which the individual attempts to assert his own creativity and achieve his own reality while social forces are constantly impinging, attempting to pervert the natural impulses and force the individual to conform to rigid standards which deny his humanity. This view decrees a constant social war in which the world is dichotomized into two kinds of people: on one side are those who are completely accepting and make no demands, who allow people to "be themselves"; on the other side are the oppressors. These latter have ulterior motives and personal integrity demands that no compromises be made with them. The free individuals can commune together while rejecting all others, a position which leads to their own general isolation. The philosophy permits maximum acceptance of in-group behaviours and maximum rejection of all others who comprise an undifferentiated out-group.

This viewpoint, while it is diffused throughout the social structure, has its sociological roots in social activities which are performed in isolation from others. The alienation of the intellectual in contemporary Western society, founded on a basic individualism, is magnified to enormous dimensions in a prison setting. Prisons, according to Friedenburg (1980), are part of the "politics of resentment". The individualistic view which sees the individual in conflict with society per se receives substantial reinforcement under conditions of imprisonment. Prisons are the most obvious expression of the coercion on which the social order is ultimately based.

As we have argued, the demand for the abolition of the prison system has been advanced by many social liberals who regard it as a "collosal mistake" and call for prisons to be "gradually torn down". The Quakers, who were instrumental in the origins of imprisonment in the 18th century, are now in the vanguard of the progressive movement to de-prison society. However laudatory the aims of these groups and individuals may be (see Cuthan 1981), the conservative response that the prison is here to stay is a powerful one. The practice of social banishment is justified in the name of social order, to protect society from dangerous individuals. More fundamentally, the needs of social control in an alienating society necessitate the maintenance of an institution which can isolate those who are threats to the social order. It is not only the ideological or symbolic importance of the prison that is at stake but its capacity for segregating and confining individuals.

The implication of recognizing the long-term stability of the prison system is to emphasize the importance of prison reform. Reform means a movement towards de-prisonization, although this unintentionally increases social control in society in general. It means the mobilization of the prison population to demand concrete reforms of prison conditions, with the crucial aspect being the process rather than achievement. Most fundamentally it means to work towards increasing the autonomy of prisoners, the scope of control they exercise over their lives, while recognizing the dual nature of such reforms and the potential for cooptation. Ultimately, however, a movement to democratize prisons must be connected with a wider political movement to democritize society. Within such a social movement, the possibility exists of both kinds of reformation: of conditions and of individuals.

Despite the persuasive depiction of prison conditions, and the delegitimization of the prison administration, staff and officialdom in general, the libertarian critique in its most extreme is actually unable to support concrete reform measures which are merely viewed one-sidely as potential pacifiers. Libertarianism acts to undermine the development of such a reform movement which, almost by definition, seeks intermediate gains and is based on an alliance with all groups and individuals who will support these concrete measures. The solution envisaged by the libertarian is individual in scope and is concerned with the "selves" of the prisoners. Rebellion is advocated, but it is rebellion against all order. The depiction of the culture of degradation forced on the prisoners by the prison itself and the acts of the brutalized staff within it leads to the conclusion that the prisoners must escape from it, that is, must pull themselves out and humanize themselves. It is in this sense that the promotion of such individual rebellion in the prison serves the short-term interests of specific prisoners, but to the extent that it diverts the response to the oppressive conditions into channels of introspective self-indulgence it inhibits the development of genuine reform sentiments in the prison.

To the extent that libertarianism and critical theory remove themselves further from the social structure, they be-

come little more than channels for individualistic self-improvement. The irony behind critical theory and the more extreme form of individual libertarianism is that they both
appear to be ultra-radical and as threatening the very fabric
of the social structure. Both, however, arise from the same
forces and divert radical response into individual posturing.
In this sense they have an element in common with anarchism
and all are ultimately supportive of the oppressive reality
they are in verbal rebellion against.

The New Rebellion

There have always been "rebellious" prisoners. Given the
nature of the social system, this is inevitable. However, the
content of this rebelliousness and its interconnections with
wider social processes have changed over time. In contrast to
the spontaneous uprising associated with the civil-rights consciousness in the 1950's, beginning about the middle 1960s in
the United States, prison riots had a distinctly different
character in that they were linked with movements and social
contradictions having their locus outside the prison. The
internal disorder expressed a greater social discontent and had
a greater progressive potential. The basic conjunctural features were the Vietnam war and the uprisings in the black
ghettos, both of which affected the consciousness of primarily
non-white prisoners who formed the leadership of the new prison
movements (Pallas and Barber 1976; Else and Stephenson 1974).
Many rebellious inmates came to define themselves as "political
prisoners". The society had given them an unequal start in the
beginning and then imprisoned them when they broke its rules
(Park 1972: 22-23).

Two inter-related factors are important in this perspective. One is the growing influence of the "community", that is,
the increasing impinging of social contradictions external to
the prison on the prisoners (contradictions which in turn
reflect on the prison itself). Second, was the changing consciousness linking the internal and external aspects. According to the prison administration, the community influence had
been expected to help change the prisoners' ideas to those
favourable to the prison staff. In the turmoil of the 1960s
and 1970s, a series of generalizations arose which asserted
that the prison played a specifically oppressive role in class
society (cf. Taylor, Walton and Young 1973). Within this new
ideology of rebellion, the rejection by the prisoners of the
prison, the security staff, and the rehabilitators was given
some articulation. At its most fully developed, this new
ideology went beyond the civil libertarian view that prisons
were wrong because they did not allow prisoners to "be themselves". In the new spirit of rebellion the "selves" of many
prisoners were transformed by the adoption of new ideological
positions. Although based on the normal conflict consciousness
which prison reproduces, the widening of this consciousness, to

the extent that it developed, did not originate in the prison but came from the outside.

The development of solidary opposition during this period was countered by a series of official measures both repressive and divisive. The opportunity exists in prison for easily isolating key individuals and dividing the rest into seemingly antagonistic groupings. Racism serves this primary function effectively and the potential perceived in the massive rebellion of state prisoners at Attica, for example, had its source partly in the multi-racial leadership (Pallas and Barber 1976). The new consciousness was still expressed in concrete demands for improved conditions which could have been met by the prison administration. The efficacy of reformism as an ideology, however, arises from the direction of change as much as from the content. The use of armed force suppresses the original movement and divisive tactics introduced as reforms shores up the legitimate channels.

The "new" penologists were liberal and sophisticated enough to understand the oppressiveness of the prison and the potential for rebellion. Their response was to give recognition to the cultural symbols of this striving and accept the principle of some delegation of decision-making to "responsible" prisoners (Wright 1976: 260). They were prepared to encourage seemingly radical programmes which would lessen the frustration and boredom of the prison regime and channel the rebellious impulses into related but "rehabilitative" activities.

Crucial to an understanding of prison reform from below is that the demands were collective in nature and if implemented would have been collective in content and could have reinforced both internal opposition and wider social connections. The nature of the conflict consciousness of the prison, however, need not induce a collective response. The oppression of the prison also provides the basis for the reinforcement of individual rebelliousness which separates prisoners from each other (cf. Colvin 1981) and, despite its appearance, acts to channel the potential for solidary opposition into the generalized rebelliousness characteristic of libertarianism, or into worse kinds or retaliatory and divisive violence against "inmate undesirables" (Desroches 1981). Most prison rebellions, then, have only the potential for developing consciousness and making wider social links. In fact this potential has seldom been realized and prison disturbances remain spontaneous outbursts caused by a combination of immediate factors on the background of a general oppression.

Conclusion

The response within penology to the social turmoil of the 1960s and the disruption of the prison took three general

forms. There was an increase in the law and order rhetoric as
conservatives declared that the rehabilitative philosophy had
made prison too soft. They demanded a return to the more
traditional prison system which at least, they claimed, knew
how to maintain order. Radical criminologists generally by-
passed the study of the prison in favour of analysing the
process by which criminality was defined by the dominant
groups. Liberal reformers, who could not countenance a return
to punishment, in the still comparatively stable social climate, devised a new series of reforms which took into account
the importance of the wider society, while catering to their
own middle class occupational interests (Ellis 1979). This new
penology made promises which were no less sweeping than the
champions of the old rehabilitation model, and it appeared that
real prison reform was on the horizon--the prison system really
could do something about crime, given the opportunity.

The older liberal reforms had not met with the success
which had been expected when they were first implemented.
Nevertheless they were not abandoned: classification, vocational training and parole all remain as institutionalized
features of the prison system. The liberal reformers may be
cynical of the extent to which these programmes contribute to
the rehabilitation of prisoners, but new life was breathed into
the old ideas when a new current of reformism occurred in the
context of the failure to rehabilitate and of radical criticism.

The new reformism was still an essentially liberal response; but it was a liberalism that claimed to be more
"realistic". Liberal reform was still ensconsed in the prison
and remained distant from the more radical-sounding critiques
while adopting their aura if not their potential substance.
While rehabilitation was rejected in some academic circles,
reforms based on the same principles continued to be
implemented.

In Canada, new programmes tend to be adopted after their
implementation elsewhere. Ironically, it is often after negative evaluations of a new reform innovation become available
that a similar programme is implemented in Canada, the result
of a considerable cultural lag. Since theory arises in
national contexts other than Canadian ones, it tends to be more
in advance of reforms instituted in this country. In the
Canadian context, the new reformism led to the development of
community correctional programmes, some examples of which will
be examined in the next chapter.

CHAPTER EIGHT

COMMUNITY CORRECTIONS

So far we have argued that a new liberal critique of the prison emerged in the 1960s which focussed on the social context of the prison and rejected the view that the prison could be studied in isolation from the society of which it was a part. The roots of the criminal processing system were questioned by a radical critique of law as demonstrating a class bias in legislation and enforcement. Criminologists and social theorists alike questioned the rehabilitation model as it had been implemented. The logic of banishment was questioned by those who took "corrections" seriously as an attempt to reform individual criminals and reintegrate them into social life. The relationships between the prison and the community were complex and problematic. A sociological study of criminality involved the question of objective processes which were connected to the creation of crime. A reemphasis on environmental causation inplied that the "community"--by which was meant the aggregate of social relationships--was at least partly responsible for the crime that was committed. The community, then, bore a responsibility to see that the criminal was reformed.

It had been assumed that the appropriate response to the criminalistic subculture within the wider society had been to isolate the offender from deleterious social influences. Within the prison, the representatives of the society and guardians of the public trust were responsible for resocializing the criminal into the norms of the outside world. The studies of the prison structure, however, had reinforced earlier beliefs that prisons deepened criminality and were schools of crime. In particular it became more apparent that the crucial independent variable in "success" had less to do with the prison experience and related more to the opportunities and options avaiable to the ex-prisoner subsequent to his release. The crucial source of re-entry difficulties had little to do with personal limitations, emotional problems or attitude, but was a question of the opportunity structure of the ex-prisoner's life situation. The ability to find a steady job was particularly important to the successful avoidance of reconviction. A return to a former life style is a functional and rational sort-term response to decarceration (McArthur 1974). The problem of employment was left in the hands of the free market, although there were some attempts at liaison with government departments responsible for employment, and some programmes employing ex-prisoners in the community were implemented. In their treatment of the employment problem, the individualistic perspective of the liberal social scientists led them to emphasize the objective skills of the ex-prisoner, and more importantly, his or her attitude and motivations. It was a case of inadequate socialization to the norms of the free community.

The belief in the efficacy of exiling the offender from the community could only be reconciled with this view of individual deficits on the assumption that it was possible to socialize an individual into a social environment while at the same time separating him from that setting. The argument that conformity to the prison regime was a process of re-socialization which was generalizable to the society outside the prison was condemned as both mistaken and ideoogical in that it justified the oppression of the prison. The prisoner, it was suggested, had to learn responsibility and this was only possible by the actual exercise of actions with a degree of autonomy, a stipulation which was thought contrary to the prison's classical emphasis on strict control. In short, there was a renewed belief in the efficacy of reformism to solve social ills, providing that they were analyzed appropriately. From the assumption that the community was partly responsible for crime, it followed that rehabilitation must take place in the community. The inherent contradiction in this view (since the community was partially responsible for crime) could be overcome depending on which experiences and guiding influences the prisoners-at-large would have in the wider society.

With the addition of a moral critique of the prison based on theories of self-actualization, a stance which underlay much of the critical writing on the prison from middle-class humanitarians, these changes portended what, in the early 1970s, was extolled as a "new revolution in corrections" (McGee 1972). The new revolution promised what the past revolutions had consistently failed to deliver: the ideal of rehabilitation, dressed in a community guise. In the United States, a massive social science research effort was mounted to uncover and remedy the malaise of the prison. Not only were improvements studied but, as McGee (1972) argued, "active attention [was paid] to new alternatives. Innovation is the magic word in applications for experimental and demonstration funds". The changes envisioned for the correctional field involved such policies as having fewer offenders incarcerated, greater emphasis on reintegration, more "work and training furloughs, weekend sentences, halfway houses, and similar community-based programs". Changes were also predicted in probabtion and parole, the integration with public and private community resources and computerized information systems "so that decision-makers throughout the justice system can operate on a basis of facts instead of opinion and guesswork". Finally, it was predicted that for the criminal who wishes "to escape the consequences of his behaviour, the 'New Correction' will be far more difficult to evade than is the case under our present system" (:xvi-xvii). In other words, the goal of rehabilitation, essentially bringing deviants to conform to the consensus, was re-affirmed and optimistically broadcast in the new wave of reform occurring at the end of the 1960s.

In 1976 Murton argued that, while past attempts at treatment "have had as their goal protection of society, punishment
of the deviant, or retribution", only recently has there been a
sincere effort at treatment. He suggests that education of
prisoners is a worthwhile objective if it is addressed (1) to
changing the attitudes of prisoners, and (2) to help them
survive in a free society. Education and training are "useful
only after the offender has changed his view of himself, his
peers, his society, and his relation to that society". He must
be willing to demonstrate self-responsibility, otherwise "the
acquisition of knowledge or skills will only enhance his compe-
tence as a criminal offender"(Murton 1976:58-59). If the
liberal reformer no longer wished to consider prisoners 'sick',
they were nevertheless still very much in need of the help
professionals could offer.

This trend to look outside the prison as well as inside,
was given official recognition in the U. S. in 1967 by the
Commission on Law Enforcement and Administration of Justice.
The theoretical basis for a trend to community corrections was
founded on the conclusion which had linked criminality to the
social structure (cf. Fitzgerald and Sim 1979: 140). The
Commission concluded that the crucial problem was the malintegration of the offender into the community: "Crime and delinquincy are symptoms of failures and organization of the community as well as of individual offenders.... The task of
corrections therefore includes building or rebuilding solid
ties between offender and community, integrating or reintegrat-
ing the offender into community life" (quoted in Richmond and
Alderhold 1972:385). In addition to changing the offender,
community institutions also needed reform. Despite this
rhetoric of "change of the community", the focus was on "integrating" into, and "mobilizing" the community--and by the "community" was meant other social agencies, whether state sponsored or middle class service organizations. The twin social
work policies of "thorough management, and control of crises
and programs designed to overcome hndicapping deficiencies"
were the suggested reformative measures (Richmond and Aderhold
1972:385).

The Ouimet Report

At about the same time the Canadian Government was summing
up the previous failures and adopting a rehabilitation model
based on the increased involvement of the community in corrections. In 1965, the Canadian Committee on Corrections was
commissioned to study the criminal justice system. This followed on the heels of the criticisms being made of prison
programmes and concern over the state of unrest in the penitentiaries. One of the main propositions of the Committee was
that the basic purpose of criminal justice was to protect all
members of society, including the offender himself, from harmful conduct (Canadian Committee on Corrections, 1969:11). In

their view, "rehabilitation of the individual offender is the best long term protection for society, since that ends the risk of a continuing criminal career" (:15).

The Ouimet Report, as this inquiry became known, outlined the trends to be followed in Canadian corrections in the late sixties as being those directed towards more citizen participation in corrections in the form of assistance from employers, labour organizations, educational institutions and volunteers, staff development through training courses in universities and community colleges, as well as the increased use of group counselling, probation and parole. The last two developments in corrections were seen by the Committee as particularly significant. Amendments in the Criminal Code in 1961 had expanded the use of probation, and by 1966, in some provinces, more adults were on probation than in prison at any given time (:36). With the establishment of a formal parole system in 1958, different kinds of programmes were being developed, including temporary leaves of absence (TLAs), day parole and work releases (cf. Porporino and Cormier 1982: 279). The system of gradual release was gaining acceptance and projects were underway for the development of standards of operation for community release centres in each of the regions to provide shelter and counselling while inmates sought employment. Financial assistance was also being granted to privately operated community release centres. Substantial resources, then, were diverted into implementing the new concept of rehabilitation.

The major recommendations made in the Ouimet Report gave legitimacy and support to the new movement for 'Community Corrections'. The Report stated that unless "there are reasons to the contrary, the correction of an offender should take place in the community, where the acceptance of a treatment relationship is more natural, where family and social relationships can be maintained" (:277). It described the necessity of the public participating in corrections, and of the offender participating in the development of a treatment plan. However, the Committee also accepted a need for prison sentences. For the majority of offenders this meant "small, specialized, community centered, appropriately staffed institutions resembling hostels or camps". For those offenders requiring incarceration, the definitions of a prison must be changed so that they were viewed as an integral part of a broad system of services within the overall correctional process and also as part of the community.

The purpose of the prison would be to hold inmates in custody for the required period and to prepare them for return to the community, that is, to "rehabilitate" them. In order to rehabilitate, an adequate treatment programme would have to be developed inside the prisons. The Ouimet Report suggested that top priority be given to the provision of adequate classification facilities, which included staff development. Also the development of the prinicple of "control through involvement rather than containment" (:308; 318), as in the concept of the therapeutic community, was given a great deal of credence. This would involve more self-determination of the inmate in treatment programme planning. The Report also encouraged the increased use of work releases for offenders to attend school, to work, or to obtain trade training in the community, and promoted the continuation of citizen participation within the institution. It recommended changes in sentencing to allow for the greater use of alternatives to imprisonment, such as proba- tion and parole. Citizen advisory committees, connected to each institution, were to be developed in order to institute the liaison and participate in the planning of programmes. The report underlined the role of the Federal government in devel- oping unity in the correctional field, and in the criminal justice system generally.

Another development in the 'Community Correction' trend, flowing from one of the recommendations in the Ouimet Report, was the creation of a Consultation Centre in 1968 within the Solicitor General's Department. The Ouimet Report called for greater federal-provincial cooperation in the area of criminal justice and for the Federal government to take on a leadership and coordinating role. The Consultation Centre constituted a move towards the development of alternatives to incarceration, toward crime prevention and community-based treatment and away from corrections inside prisons. The main priority groups were young people and special interest groups such as Native Peoples. A second objective of the Centre was to continue public participation in corrections in the form of voluntary organizations working with offenders and ex-offenders, private sector input into policy-making and the promotion of experimen- tation within community programmes. Projects were funded which provided some diversion and preventive services. For a while, Community Residential Centres (CRCs) were granted money by the Centre but later the Centre declined to fund this type of alternative.

The tendency seems to be to support a project for a limited time and then to drop support and look elsewhere be- cause the continuation of funding creates a "permanent need". One of the areas which has not been a priority has been the period subsequent to the granting of parole. An organization called Coalition and Support Service (CSS) was developed in one locality to employ ex-prisoners in projects which assisted the disadvantaged in the Community. Called "the most effective and best directed" project in Canada by a senior civil servat in the Solicitor General's Department, the programme had been funded by Government sponsored make-work projects such as LIP and LEAP. Despite its excellent record, however, it fell victim to the cutbacks and the policy of avoiding long-term commit- ments. The Solicitor General's Department offered an amount of money representing about eight per cent of the budget, but

declined to become seriously involved in a project which focussed on the decarceration period.

The goal of treatment was the successful re-integrating of
the ex-offender into the society. To have more control over
this transition, the establishment of intermediate prisons, or
halfway houses was suggested. The prison counsellors and
guards were no longer seen as acceptable surrogates for the
inculcation of middle class norms and values, at least as these
norms were ideally pictured, including autonomy and decision-
making power. They were more appropriate for the inculcation of
blind obedience and deference to authority. We have questioned
how realistic these assumptions of middle class reformers were,
as reflected in the attempt to set up "therapeutic communities"
in which people openly discuss their problems and ideas and
arrive at collective decisions. Despite the rhetoric this
model never has been an accurate reflection of decision-making
in Western society. Nevertheless, the view that you cannot
isolate an individual from a social environment and simultan-
eously socialize him to that environment was coupled with the
empirical finding that a crucial determinant of reconviction
was employment record following release, combined to enhance
the prisoner's need to develop a conventional role in the "free
society". The prison had been expected to train the prisoner
in marketable skills; the halfway house was to assist the
individual in testing the new role and supposedly initiating
"rewarding experiences which would tie him to the new role."

As they have currently been instituted, halfway houses
meet only a small percentage of the demand. The recognition of
a problem and its posited solution within the framework of
reform becomes mere tokenism by the failure to implement the
programme widely and thereby meet the needs recognized in
theory. This is not to imply that the reforms themselves may
not be fundamentally problematic, but rather to stress the
further point that the implementation of policies which are
thought to be positive is directly related to political and
economic considerations. This includes the appropriation of
necessary funds, a factor which is ultimately dependent on the
aggregate of public monies available to the state for reformative purposes. The trend towards community corrections occurred in a specific conjuncture when more money was made available to the Departments of Justice and of the Solicitor General. While the amount of money allocated may be regarded as one
form of basic datum, a second issue is the allocation of this
money. Here political and ideological considerations play a
considerable part.

The development of community corrections took three institutional forms: the provision of alternative medium security
prisons, an increased supervision of ex-prisoners in the community, and some modest revisions of programmes in the standard
prison system. A considerable amount of attention was focussed

on the first two aspects, leading to the expansion of institutions of both a pre-release and a post-release nature. The
explicit aim was to provide a more controlled re-integration
into the community in the hope that this would lead to an
increased success rate for parolees. Mere supervision was
deemed insufficient; there was an attempt to intervene more
positively in the process of re-integration. The implementation of this aspect of the "new revolution" in corrections was
examined by a Task Force commissioned for the purpose of evaluation. The outcome was the Outerbridge Report which reinforced
the trend towards community corrections by supporting the concept of post-release Community Residential Centres.

Community Residential Centres

The Outerbridge Report came out in full support of the
idea of community responsibility for crime and "Community Corrections". The Report declared that "most criminal conduct is
spawned in the community, contributed to by the social, economic and political circumstances of the community. Thus, criminal behaviour is a function both of the offender and of the
community, and the solutions must be sought in both" (Task
Force 1972:28). It agreed with the prevailing view in corrections at that time that prisons had failed (:30). It argued
that prisons did not protect society, except in the short-term
sense. For the "majority of offenders, community-based aterna-
tives to conventional forms of imprisonment should be maximized" (:31). "Community Corrections" was seen as only part of
a broad social movement to change policies in the administration of criminal justice. Decriminalization of certain acts,
detoxification centres, bail hostels, increased use of probation and fines, payment of restitution and partial prison
sentences were some of the reforms measures advocated. Where
imprisonment was deemed necessary, the task force stressed the
use of minimum institutions and the maximum use of parole and
other forms of early release.

This concept entailed developing alternatives to imprisonment which would divert persons from the criminal justice
system, shorten the length of incarceration or bring relief
from incarceration through temporary leaves of absences, day
paroles, weekend sentences and work releases. Most community
residential centres (CRCs) accepting ex-offenders opened in the
early years of the trend. At the time of the Report, 156
centres were available (Task Force 1972: 10). There are a
variety of different kinds of CRCs, ranging from residences
which provide purely overnight accommodation to those providing
long-term residence with special programmes of varying intensities. These included long-standing halfway houses for alcoholics and drug addicts as well as for transients.There seems to
be a great deal of experimentation in organization and treatment styles. However, most centres attempt to provide a 'home'
atmosphere which would include a meal programme. Some involve

inmates in the determination and implementation of programmes, while others have compulsory treatment and counselling. The rules and principles in most CRCs are established by the director. Most are understaffed because of the demanding hours. Staff training consists of weekly staff meetings to discuss problems. Many ex-offenders are entering the CRC movement and creating self-help groups. One major complaint from administrators is a lack of communication between CRCs. There are few formal mechanisms for coordination of activities and for information exchange between institutions. Most of the available beds exist in the accommodation-only centres. Halfway houses which serve as post-release centres are all operated by the private sector. The government grants subsidies to these centres but is not involved in operating them. Most of them are old homes and tend to have low-key programmes which place few demands on the residents.

The second main type of CRC is the alcohol and drug treatment centres. The drug treatment programmes are usually of a communal and intense nature, requiring total involvement and a lengthy stay. Various techniques are used such as traditional psychotherapy, both on an individual and group basis, and newer methods such as psychodrama, marathon encounter groups and Gestalt therapy. The alcohol treatment programmes generally are less intense, requiring a shorter stay and follow the Alcoholics Anonymous philosophy.

The Task Force was asked to investigate CRCs in Canada and lay down some guiding principles and standards for them, as well as recommend the nature of the role of the Federal government in relation to the centres. The task force found that there were no commonly accepted standards for CRCs and that all empirical studies to date on the subject were insufficient for the development of standards of evaluation to be created. The Report argued that the effectiveness of CRCs in comparison with other alternatives could not yet be measured (Task Force 1972:12). In its view, however, the single criterion of recidivism should not be the sole element used in evaluation, and a calculation of the social and economic costs to society should also be included.

The Task Force discovered that most CRCs were not filled to capacity partly because ex-prisoners did not know that CRCs existed in the area in which they were to be released. Their usual source of information was ex-offenders on the street. It also found that most CRCs were unhappy with the contractual agreements with the Solicitor General's Department according to which $10 per day per referral was paid to selected CRCs. If a bed was not filled, no payment would be made. CRCs did receive funding through other government sources, and the task force estimated that 38.5 per cent of CRCs funds come from Federal sources. The cost of operating pre-release centres was found to be about twice as much as post-release centres, $21.29 per diem as opposed to $10.39 (:24). As one consequence of these perennial funding problems, a number of CRCs began to accept non-offenders in order to widen potential funding sources.

The Outerbridge Report recommended the expansion of CRCs viewing them as viable alternatives to incarceration. It recommended that CRCs should be small, autonomous, innovative and creative, with informal and personal orientation for inmates and a high degree of resident participation. Arguments were made that an increased number of CRCs would lessen overcrowding in penitentiaries, where the population had been rising since the mid-1960s, and would lessen the need for construction of new institutions. Probation and parole had served this purpose earlier but, according to the task force, they appeared to have reached a peak at that time. It was recommended that CRCs offer different programmes and services in varying intensities to meet individual needs. Staff development would be a priority, with training courses becoming available in universities and community colleges, and through in-service training. In order to encourage innovation and experimentation, the Report suggested that standards of evaluation should be kept to a minimum to allow for the growth of the movement. Some type of national forum should be set up for the exchange of ideas and as a mechanism for coordination. The Federal Government was counselled to take an active role in the growth and development of CRCs.

The CRC was designed for the ex-convict who is on either full parole or mandatory supervision, but is regarded as not ready to be independent on the street. The CRC is the cheapest institution available for offenders and has the smallest staff/parolee ratio. Only direct parole supervision and probation are cheaper. The tendency has been to expand the CRCs, but not to give priority to the development of a second form of institution concerned with the release period, the Community Correctional Centre. In practice, the CRC has generally become only a new form of warehouse which provides nothing more than a bed and a place to eat for parolees. As usual, the outcome of policy recommendations is the implementation of the minimal possible reforms.

Community Correctional Centres

The pre-release centres of the traditional halfway house type are federally operated and are called Community Correctional Centre (CCCs). The Canadian Peniteniary Service (CPS) began to provide CCCs in the late 1960s, stemming from a recommendation of the Ouimet Report which focused on the post-release problem. The first three CCCs were established in Toronto, Winnipeg and Vancouver and it was expected at the time that CCCs would spread across the country. They were expected to have multiple roles, and to house inmates prior to the expiry of their sentence, suspended parolees as an alternative to their re-imprisonment, as well as prisoners on temporary leaves of absence or day parole. In general, inmates are expected to apply for this programme, although the ultimate decision of eligibility is made by the National Parole Board because most prisoners need some form of parole to leave the prisons. However, directors of the centres make recommendations on specific individuals. Programmes at CCCs may consist of weekly compulsory meetings of residents and staff which air complaints and provide group counselling, although individual counselling is available on request. Considerable attention is given to providing assistance for ex-offenders who are seeking to obtain employment in the community. Within the CCC, rules are laid down regarding unacceptable conduct, hours, drugs, and alcohol. The ultimate sanction is to return the prisoner to a medium or maximum prison.

The 12 CCCs in Canada are each different from the other, the variation of physical plant depending on the actual architecture of the building. The types of programmes vary according to these restraints as well as according to the correctional philosophy held by the director and staff. In Saint John, the CCC is on the top floor of the YMCA and is quite limited in its facilities; the CCC in Edmonton was described as more like a medium security prison. The characteristics of the community in which the centre is located has an important influence in shaping both the style of the CCC as well as its programme, since it functions as a facility for parolees who by definition spend their day-time in the community. The building of CCCs has not been made a Government priority. Its potential for forming an alternative to the regular prisons by having convicted offenders sent directly to the CCC has not been realized. The Atlantic region tends to look favourably on the CCCs and would like to expand them; however, the national priority is more towards the less expensive CRCs which supposedly provide basic physical amenities and serve as a stop-gap between the prison and the community, but do not concenrate on rehabilitation which is meant to be provided in the CCCs. The CCC concept has not been extinguished, however, and the existing centres are continuing to function.

In theory the CCC has no control over the selection of parolees who come to the Centre. For each specific case, the issue arises in the maximum or minimum prison upon the application of a prisoner for day parole. This application is sent down for a community assessment as part of the review process. The staff of the CCC evaluates the potential parolee and submits a report which, in the case of a negative recommendation, states reasons for the rejection. According to the administration of one Centre, this gives them, in practice, control over who comes to the CCC since there have been no cases in which the decision has gone contrary to their recommendation.

According to CCC administrative personnel interviewed, no

one should be excluded from the CCC on the basis of having a
low probability of success. The staff, it was stated, will
work with anyone who is in need of the facilities the Centre
can offer, or who can be helped. Besides the question of needs
and resources, the effect of the social climate of the Centre
on the individual prisoner is taken into consideration: this
includes the reaction to close supervision, potential problems
living with other parolees, their reaction to restrictions, and
so on. It was explicitly denied that selection has anything to
do with the prisoner's probability of success (although those
who are considered "criminally engrained" are excluded), and it
was stated that parolees would be taken if their needs were
acute even if it was suspected that they would not work out
well, because their need was acute. To accept parolees on a
probability basis would mean accepting only "good risks", but
the administrators claimed that their policy was to accept
those who are not good risks if they concluded that, with the
addition of the resources and support of the Centre, the
parolees could be more successful in the community. However,
in this evaluation, the question of a parolee's security risk--
whether he or she was thought to be dangerous to the public--is
paramount. The prisoner's criminal record, as well as such
intangibles as a psychological/psychiatric profile, and the
"ability to cope with stress" are included in the evaluation,
both with respect to concern for the safety of the community
and the continued existence of the Centre itself.

The crucial contradiction in the selection arises in the
distinction between what is defined as the ex-offender's need
for the resources of the Centre, and the question of whether
the experience can be expected to be reformative. According to
the administrator of one CCC, if the prison system had a potential parolee who was thought to have "nothing going for him"
then the Parole Board would approach the Centre and request
that this individual be placed. However, the local administrators could reject the parolee on the grounds that his or her
specific needs could not be met by the resources of the CCC.
In this way some particularly problematic individuals can be
excluded from the programme. Similarly, if the security risk,
or the assumed degree to which an ex-offender is deemed a
danger to society, can be considered analogous to a negatively
ordered probability of success scale, then by definition the
Centre accepts those least liable to commit infractions for
which they would be re-incarcerated. Despite this potential
for a bias in selection, the actual outcome suggests that the
administrators may be correct in their claims that they do not
choose participants on the basis of their probability of success. Research indicates that the CCC is no more successful
than a random sample of matched prisoners parolled without the
benefits of a pre-release centre (Murphy 1984).

When they were first opened, some CCCs were operated on
the principles of behaviour modification. This philosophy

asserted that it was possible to rehabilitate someone whether they wanted it or not. Upon first entering the CCC the parolee had no privileges; subsequently these benefits could be earned. The parolees were evaluated periodically on such things as their attitude, cleanliness, and so on, and awarded points for good behaviour. The number and kind of privileges which a parolee was entitled to depended on his "grade" which was based on the accumulation of points. The marks were posted periodically and the result was a great deal of negative competition among parolees about relative marks which had of necessity a large subjective element. This type of programme was consistent with the philosophy of rehabilitation and with the correctional approach of the administrator in charge at the time.

At present this system of rewards and punishments is not generally used. More commonly now, some basic privileges are extended to all parolees and are withdrawn upon misbehaviour, a reversal of the "positive reward" philosophy which shapes behaviour modification. This policy is continued with regard to daily passes, which can be issued for as long as from 6:00 a.m. to midnight on weekdays, to 1:00 a.m. on weekends. During the first two months the parolee is eligible for one weekend pass. Thereafter the number of weekend passes per month for which a parolee is eligible increases, these passes being "granted on the basis of.....progress". The passes are privileges and not rights, and the Parole Service must do a Community Assessment before a pass will be granted for a specific individual and a specific place.

One principle underlying the handling of parolees in some Centres is an individual programme planning model. When the parolee enters the centre, a programme of activity is worked out together with the counsellors and senior staff. The first two weeks are used for orientation during which needs and potential resources are identified. This is defined as a "structured period" during which supervision is a relative priority and privileges are few. Depending on a "progress" evaluation by the Centre and the Parole Service, either the orientation will continue or the parolee can transfer to a regular programme. It is expected that during the initial meeting a clear outline of expectations will be established in a contractual process, in which objectives are outlined. These objectives are set out in a formal agreement and may consist of areas related to job search, personal habits, cleaning duties, and the like. Such agreements are viewed as being binding and while the terms may be reconsidered by mutual consent, failure to work toward the goals that are outlined may result in termination of day parole. The usual objective is release, or full parole through a CRC, and the time in the CCC can help in two ways: just by participating in the programme the parolee is expected to actively change him or herself; second, by appearing to participate in the programme, the probability of success with the parole board is enhanced.

The programme worked out is based on some correspondence between what are identified as the needs of the parolee and what the resources of the community are which can go some way to meeting these needs. The Centre itself usually does not attempt to provide a full range of specific programmes. It does provide bed and board, some individual and group counselling, leisure activities, as well as some organization which attempts to realize the potential for a collective responsibility among the prisoners for shared day-to-day activities. There is generally less effort to provide group events, such as a collective visit to a theatrical performance. Rather than primarily providing services itself, the Centre attempts to assist the parolee's use of as many community services as possible. These include the YMCA, Manpower, Social Servics, religious organizations, the John Howard Society, prospective employers, Commissions on Drug Dependency, and whatever other government or private community agencies are available and useful in the individual case. It is difficult to generalize to all of the CCCs since the type of internal programme is dependent on the resources available to the Director and the staff as well as the philosophy guiding the administration. These can vary widely in detail from setting to setting.

One of the voluntary treatment programmes which is currently used in some CCCs is based on the concept of "life skills", which can be considered the contemporary term for inadequate socialization, and is defined as a crucial problem for the prisoners. Some parolees in the Centre prove to be functionally illiterate, and attend manpower training courses, but the concept of "life skills" is much broader and social in its scope and pertains to the most basic levels of social relationships: the ability to eat well, to "survive on their own", "the ability to feel comfortable walking around the block", and so on, all of which are defined as "survival skills". Some have difficulty facing such situations as a job interview, with which a great deal of anxiety and tension is connected. The parolees are thought to be unaware of the expectations that people in positions of power or authority place on them.

The technique is to define such "social skills" and then have the prisoners practice them in the group setting with the expectation that they will feel more comfortable in similar situations with strangers. The basic areas in which the Life Skills programmes work are the family, the self, work and leisure. One staff member would be trained in the imparting of "life skills", which could also form part of the orientation to the Centre. Originally set up as a demonstation project, it was found that there was some difficulty getting parolee's commitment to the life skills concept. By moving this programme to the initial trial period, when the parolee can more easily be sent back to the prison, the institution relies on the desire of the parolee to gain the privileges promised by the Centre.

The problems of administering a CCC are made more difficult in certain respects because of the proximity of the
prisoners to the community. The potential for obtaining items
regarded by the staff as illicit, and bringing them into the
Centre, is one internal problem especially endemic to the
minimum security CCC. What happens both in the institution and
in the case of those on parole is that a certain amount of
contraband is deemed permissible by those in authority, not in
the sense that they explicitly legitimize it, but from the
point of view that they consider constant intervention to be
impractical and undesirable. In practice, for example, no
drugs or other contraband are permitted in the Cente, and
bringing them in or possessing drugs is sanctioned by penalties
which could amount to termination of the day parole and the
laying of criminal charges. The decision on such action is the
joint responsibility of the Director of the Centre and the
District Director of the National Parole Service. It could be
settled then, either as an internal house affair or as a criminal matter. It was suggested by the staff that to maintain a
hard and fast line would be extremely difficult and would
actually undermine the work that the Centre tries to do.

This question involves accepting certain behaviours of the
parolee as a condition for the parolee's compliance with the
staff in their attempt to conduct counselling. The antagonism
is there, not only in the rules which the staff are expected to
police, but in the power of the ultimate sanction of the
Centre--return to the maximum prison, coupled with a negative
report making the attainment of privileges in the future more
difficult. In order to achieve some cooperation, then, a
pragmatic view of certain violations is essential. In the
maximum or medium prison, prisoners' use of contraband serves
what has been regarded as the latent function of providing the
prisoners with leisure activities, sensory experiences, and an
acceptable way to handle situations of intense stress. In
short, that it serves to increase social control along the
classical lines of literary science fiction.

The philosophy of the CCC is now consistent with the view
which places responsibility on the parolees. This, as we will
argue in the next chapter, is the current 1980s ideology of
corrections in Canada. The administrators in the CCC were
explicit that the facilities of the Centre are not for everyone, but only for those who apply for it, meet the criteria and
are accepted. This need for a formal choice by a prisoner
makes it similar to the therapeutic community. The Centre,
however, places less emphasis on taking authority away. The
counsellors claim that they attempt to break down some of the
barriers between themselves and the staff, and overcome some of
the negative experiences of the parolees in their prison
history, but they do not assume that it is possible to estab-

lish an equal relationship between those with and those without
formal power. Ideologically, the exercise involves the attempt
to convince the parolee that his own best interests are served
by cooperation with the staff. Little time is provided for the
development of this rapport, however, since the average length
of stay in the Centre is about four to six months.

Many prisoners prefer to be left alone for the duration of
the sentence, but this is deemed to be "systematically negative"; the CCC is described as a "valuable bed" and is not for
isolated non-involvement. The Centre is for parolees who
recognize that they have problems and are willing to try to
"work on them". The CCC provides a voluntary program of academic up-grading, life skills and work, and the parolee is
expected to have chosen rehabilitation rather than "marking
time". The typical response involved in gaining insights into
one's behaviour may be represented by a prisoner from central
Canada who asked for release in a different community because
if he went back to his old city the same things would happen to
him again. He expressed a fatalism associated with his
environmental influences in addition to a naive hope that
something could be done to help him. The CCC has many desirable features relative to the rest of the penitentiary system
in Canada. It does attempt to meet an important need of ex-
offenders. It remains, however, an anomaly because the government has not expanded the programme at the same time as CCCs
slowly degenerate into residential units rather than helping
institutions.

Community Corrections and the Prison

The philosophy of the new community-based reformism was
reflected above all in alternatives to incarceration, as well
as the development of pre- and post-release centres. The
prison, however, remained the basic punitive cum rehabilitative
institution in the system and the trend to community corrections also affected the development of institutional programmes. In the late 1960s Dorchester Penitentiary was described
as having a relatively active programme of rehabilitation.
There was some limited participation in the community by some
inmates although the major early emphasis was to bring groups
or organizations from the community into the prison. But as
Dorchester's role became more explicitly a maximum prison, and
high security risks were sent for warehousing, the programmes
in the prison declined.

The change at Springhill, from a prison designated primarily for youths and first convictions to a standard medium, had
not been merely a case of conflicting objectives in Dorchester
and Springhill but was also affected by plans at the national
level. The severe problem of overcrowding, particularly in
British Columbia, had precipitated the predictable disturbances, so the shift of medium security prisoners to Springhill

was followed by the transfer of a large draft consisting of
about 150 prisoners from the B. C. penitentiary system in 1971-
72. The total population of the prison was raised to between
450 and 480. This change in the number and composition of the
prison population at first reinforced the tendency in Dorchester to let fewer prisoners out into the community. Few of the
prisoners remaining in Dorchester were able to meet the requirements for temporary leaves of absence.

The policy of cutting back on TLAs also resulted from more
widespread political considerations. According to prison
administrators, by 1973 the policy of granting such leaves was
cut back as a result of the arousal of negative public opinion
brought about by a number of well publicized incidents in which
crimes were committed by people temporarily released. The
benefits of the programme for those who did not create trouble
were lost in the view that prisoners should not be let out
early because they were in prison to be punished for previous
crimes. The view of the correctional officials was that
parolees had managed to escape part of their rightful punishment. The upshot of this adverse publicity was that TLAs became
increasingly difficult to obtain. Prisoners were less able to
go into the community in order to be resocialized. At best
energies were to be directed into encouraging programmes which
could be brought into the prison.

In 1968 a community service group began to sponsor self-
development training programmes for prisoners in Dorchester in
such areas as speech-making and leadership skills. In the
beginning, the programme attracted what the treatment staff
described as the "better type" of prisoner, meaning the kind
who would not strain at the bit. Following the removal from
Dorchester to Springhill of many prisoners defined as medium
security risks, however, a new executive of the service programme was instituted. They were described by the staff as
"hard-core types" who wanted to use the organization to press
demands for reforms. That is, from an individual training
programme devoted to self-improvement, the executive attempted
to transform the programme into a device for organizing prisoners and working for the redress of grievances, for an increased
number of TLAs, increased visiting privileges, and other reforms. They tried to function as a "union" for prisoners. In
the words of the staff, they had become a new "power group" in
the prison.

The inevitable showdown occurred and the service programme
had to be "reorganized". The leadership was changed and it was
again run by a "more realistic" and "more select" group of
inmates. The group was given some control over its membership.
It could decide such questions as the number of members and the
length and frequency of meetings. The group also provides its
own "ways and means" by engaging in such activities as selling
valentine cards and chocolates to raise money. The organiza-

tion, particularly through the agency of community liaison, is permeated by the liberal ideology of small scale business.

In its Accent on Youth programme, members of the service group went out to high schools and told the students their life stories. The basic line was: "I've been down the road--don't follow me". During one year this message was brought to 60,000 students and was described as being a very rewarding experience for the prisoners, who had to articulate their understanding of how they had gotten where they were. This involved accepting the individualistic perspective according to which they were responsible for their own imprisonment and were receiving the social condemnation they deserved. These prisoners represent the philosophy of rehabilitation with its legitimation of the social structure and of the prison within it. They are the successes who have been transformed (at least temporarily) into non-criminals who counsel others that the question of crime lies in individual hands and that there are always legitimate opportunities. Like the religious penitent, the fully rehabilitated man is able to espouse the dominant ideology which reinforces the dichotomy between criminals and non-criminals.

The basic assumption underlying these types of programmes (social development in general, life skills, group therapy) is that there is some relationship between the observed inadequacies in the prison population and what is considered to be their criminality. However, there is no necessary connection-- the problems associated with so-called cultural deprivation (the application of middle class standards to working class families) are social in origin and widespread, and similar types of programmes are offered by other service groups in the community as well as federal departments such as Manpower. But if these programmes in prison do not address criminality, even in their own terms, then it is hardly surprising that recidivism remains a major problem.

The primary point to be made is that the most idealistic liberal view of rehabilitation also involves an attempt at ideological transformation, only in this case it is less realistic in content. The prisoner, like the "mental patient" who must first admit to being "ill", must come to understand his own individual inadequacies. The society is just and the distribution of rewards is contingent upon hard work and good behaviour and it is by accepting these values that successful rehabilitation can occur. If in fact the vast majority of inmates fail to evolve a new perspective on their society, this is not because such a transformation is impossible but rather because this view is not an accurate reflection of experienced reality and cannot compete with the less formal ideology of prison life with its explicit subcultural jargon and implicit rebellion against authority.

114

Conclusion

It appears that the new reform wave based on increased community involvement is going the way of all past reform. While arising as a response to the salutary idea that sees crime as having its causes in society in general, the actual operation of the new programmes leaves the central institutional structure of the society intact. What is called "community involvement" in the new reform is nothing more than the attachment of new administrative units onto the same old prison (cf. Native Counselling Services of Alberta 1982: 327). Moreover, one of the consequences of the movement has been to increase the degree of social control in the society as a whole (Trepanier 1981). At best the new programmes end up attempting what all older reforms had also tried with little success--to rehabilitate the individual offender. The illusion that crime can be prevented by altering the behaviour of individuals who have been apprehended is one of the basic fallacies of the rehabilitative ideal.

Even if this concept of corrections were sound, the use of a reform to solve a general social problem is limited by the economic resources available, both with regard to absolute amounts and priorities. The programme flounders when it is swamped by additional numbers it cannot support, when the necessary resources cannot be maintained or when priorities change. While looking good on paper, the reform is not generalized to the prison population and handles only a small proportion of those actually in need.

Connected with the question of limited resources is the issue of administrative convenience. A rehabilitative reform, such as the Therapeutic Community or the CCC is devised and implemented as an experimental programme. Because of policy priorities elsewhere, the fundamental preconditions for success, even as these are outlined in the official literature, are soon violated. Financial pressure on the remaining facilities caused by a commitment of resources for what appears to be a rehabilitative frill, becomes regarded as an intolerable burden. The experiment is not extended in its original form, but a substantially modified version is generalized to the prison population as a whole. The living unit programme incorporates some of the aspects of the therapeutic community, particularly those which increase the probability (in normal circumstances) of controlling the routine functioning of the prison. The CCCs are thought to be a good idea, but the CRCs are ear-marked for expansion. They are less expensive and provide little more than housing for the early period of decarceration.

The rehabilitative programme is in the process of being abandoned in the interests of maximizing control and minimizing expense. There is a basis in reality for the liberal claim

that the rehabilitative philosophy has not been taken seriously. But this is predicated by the essential flaw in the philosophy of individual rehabilitation as a solution to crime (or
even as personal transformation in the present social climate),
and by the impracticality of its thorough implementation. The
amount of economic resources which would be necessary to correct social problems in the present social structure, in such a
way that precluded a major institutional change, is probably
out of proportion to the ability of the system to allocate
funds even in periods of relative prosperity.

In the context of a declining economy in the late 1970s
and early 1980s, the concern with the failure to rehabilitate
began to give way in official circles to the view that rehabilitation as a concept had failed. What would be predicted in
such a social climate is that traditional punitive assumptions
easily flow in to fill the breach. In the context of a Liberal
government, however, even a return to more conservative principles must be disguised by talk and of some degree of implementation of reform.

CHAPTER NINE

THE OPPORTUNITIES PRINCIPLE: CONSERVATISM IN REFORM GUISE

The Failure of Rehabilitation

Optimism about the second wave of rehabilitation, the trend towards community corrections, was of relatively short duration. By the middle 1970s this attempt to devise programmes to correspond with the latest ideology in corrections had been declared a failure. The official conclusions had been based on the growing number of studies which rejected the rehabilitation concept in practice and as ideology. As usual, recidivism statistics were used to demonstrate the ineffectiveness of programmes. According to figures published by the Solicitor General's Department, only 20 percent of admissions to federal prisons in Canada were first offenders, and 80 percent of reconvicted offenders were free 18 months or less. The Director of Prince Albert Penitentiary declared that "the recidivism rate doesn't seem to have changed much in the last 100 years" (Ellis 1974). The basic point of rehabilitation had been to transform prisoners into law-abiding citizens, and the belief that there was virtually no relationship between treatment programme and recidivism was advanced as a justification for scrapping programmes. The implications were clear: "If what happened in penal institutions had no effect upon subsequent recidivism, what was the point of elaborate and expensive attempts to match individuals to treatment?" (Trasler 1972 :131; cf. Gibbons 1960; Outerbridge 1968).

In addition to the question of the ineffectiveness of treatment programmes, it was further argued that treatment was "coercive in character" and was administered by a staff which existed in a conflictual relationship with the prisoners (Bishop 1974:96-97; cf. Warren 1977). Two conclusions were drawn, one in the realm of ideology, and the other with respect to implementation. The understanding of the "failure of rehabilitation" was sought in the appropriation by the correctional system, of goals which were the province of the individual. As Trasler articulated this view, the "notion that the correctional system ought to aim to 'straighten' the offender, to remedy all his weaknesses, to refurbish his values, his attainments, his social skills and his spiritual responsiveness", had been refuted. In its place was "a more modest and practical goal: endeavouring to avoid further criminal reconviction" (1972: 132).

For a variety of reasons, having less to do with a scientific appraisal of the rehabilitation model and more to do with the ideological climate, the new philosophy of deterrence through incapacitation (Cousineau and Plecas 1982) appealed to conservatives in the criminal justice field. A Commissioner of Corrections in the United States was quoted as asserting that "the rehabilitative approach to imprisonment, the whole framework of indeterminate sentencing, education and job training in prison and, finally, parole have provided a structure on which prisoners outwit the people who imprison them and gain an easier time in prison and earlier release than society expects". The result was simply a "facade of public protection" (New York Times 1 June 1976). Prisoners had agreed to participate in the treatment programmes solely for instrumental reasons, principally to impress the parole board, and resumed their criminal activity upon release. The logical outcome of this argument was to curtail many of the programmes introduced into the prison systems during the post-1945 decades and to promote a greater emphasis on punishment. As a Conservative Member of Parliament in Britain declared on the BBC: serving a prison term had become a badge of honour, and something needed to be done to counter the "arrogance and pride" of prisoners. Far from being convinced that they had sinned by their penitentiary experience, prisoners were refusing to change their personalities to suit the requirements of the rehabilitators.

This attack on rehabilitation coincided with the policy of austerity implemented most consistently in Britain and the United States as a response to the fiscal crisis of the 1980s, which took a considerable toll on social programmes. Although the right-wing demands for more "law and order" imply the expansion of the "punishment industry" (Friedenberg 1980), within corrections the first place to cut back was in the new reform programmes, the most expendable frill in the budget. The days when prison was described as being less for the purpose of punishment and more for rehabilitation were gone, to be replaced by a more "realistic" appraisal. Within the overall context of the contemporary economic crisis, the new "revolution" in penology has generally undermined rehabilitation and underscored a return to a law and order perspective in the popluation expressed in a political rhetoric demanding the restoration of capital punishment, more harsh punishments for major drug offences, and in general a reiteration of the punitive model. Rehabilitation was no longer considered a realistic goal for any but a very few prisoners: for the prison administration, the goal was restricted to safe confinement of offenders.

In Canada, the Solicitor-General's Department did not abandon its concern for rehabilitation, although it was no longer the priority nor the main legitimation of the prison system. Sound correctional programmes were listed behind "necessary control [and] humane treatment" as the goals of imprisonment. It was not only, or even primarily, the academic or moral critiques of the prison that fostered a

return to conservative principles. Practical developments in
the prisons themselves reinforced a return to the "stick" of
law and order. At the same time, however, arguments from
government departments in Canada were also rallied on the
"carrot" side of the controversy. The Liberal government issued a bewildering array of liberal and conservative documents,
including the Charter of Rights and Freedoms on the one hand,
and a new Security Bill, which came in for sustained criticism
from civil libertarian lobbies, on the other (Taylor 1984).
Within the penitentiary system the main reform considerations
addressed were the civil rights of prisoners and the need for
some mechanisms to protect these rights.

The concern for prisoners rights did not arise solely
from the benevolence of the government but, in part, from the
demands of prisoners' rights groups. This development of
special interest groups for prisoners was considerably more
significant in Europe than Canada. In England the main national
group was the Preservation of the Rights of Prisoners (PROP),
which had been modelled after similar groups in the Scandinavian countries (Evans 1980: 66). After a full decade of rehabilitation, during which the prisoners had been relatively
quiescent, there was an increase in prison rebellions in North
America and in Europe. In Canada, as in the United States and
Britain (King and Morgan 1980: 5-6), disturbances and hostage-
taking incidents were occurring in the penitentiaries with
unprecedented frequency. From 1970 to 1975, there were 38
hostage-taking incidents in Canadian penitentiaries (Department
of Solicitor General 1976:55). There were just as many in 1976
alone, most of them occurring in maximums (Enright 1977:32).
In May 1971 a major riot had occurred at Kingston Penitentiary
during which six guards were taken hostage, $300,000 worth of
damage was incurred, one inmate was killed and 15 injured.
Causes of the uprising included prisoners' concern over transfer to the new Millhaven facilities and the dehumanizing routine. During the rebellion, a prisoner's committee had asked
to meet with a citizen's group to air their demands; however,
the Solicitor General would not bargain and the Armed Forces
were called in to restore order. When a settlement was reached
the officials promised that dissenters would not be abused
physically. However, when prisoners were later transferred to
Millhaven, the "ringleaders" were made to run the gauntlet
(Time 3 May 1971). It was a Canadian dress rehearsal for the
1972 events in Attica.

Underlying the move towards the justification of more
authoritarian measures in the prison was a change in the organizational style of some of the prison rebellions. Major demonstrations in Canadian penitentiaries in the mid-1970s did not
consist only of spontaneous uprisings conducted by "irrational"
prisoners lashing out at their oppressors, but there were also
some demonstrations and sit-down strikes which were well organized and generally self-controlled. In these instances,

prisoners demanded reasonable reforms such as better living
conditions, access to media, and the promise that there would
be no reprisals (MacLeans 18 October 1976). These demonstrations, however, were always close to the edge of violence, as
would be expected in a prison setting. As both conditions of
violent rebelliousness and political demands co-existed, and as
prisoners become more sophisticated politically and used the
reform ideology to achieve some of their reformist aims, the
prison system chose to resort to force to restore the power of
the administration. When it comes to a question of real power,
the prisoners are at an enormous disadvantage vis a vis government resources.

A Commission of Inquiry, which was struck to investigate
this disturbance, concluded that many of the demands of the
rioting prisoners were justified and many inmate grievances
were well founded. It listed among the "shortcomings" of the
penitentiary the aged facilities, the overcrowding, misclassi-
fication, too much time in the cells, the absence of effective
channels for grievances, a poor staff attitude, the lack of
adequate staff and an inconsistent and unstable enforcement of
regulations. Almost 35 years previously the Archambault Report
had said the same things: prison reform was still not a
reality.

The critique of rehabilitation advanced by the most conservative in the correctional field usually fails to distinguish one key function of the treatment staff which had nothing
to do with the main liberal ideology supportive of their programmes. Donald Cressey has acknowledged that the treatment
staff are employed to assist in the maintenance of control in
the prison. He regards the professional staff as serving the
function of diminishing group violence and helping to pacify
incensed prisoners (1972:440-441). By canalizing violence and
presenting an ideology of either neutrality or of acting in the
interests of the prisoners, the treatment staff attempte to
interfere with processes which polarize the prison into a
keeper/prisoner confrontation. As Martinson put it, by and
large the treatment philosophy kept the lid on for two decades,
but prison rebellions in the 1970s served to warn that it could
do so no longer (1972:17-19). The failure of rehabilitation,
then, was a double failure: not only had it failed according to
its own precepts, but it had failed in its latent function as
well. Rehabilitation was jettisoned (or rather redefined) when
it ceased to service the second function.

The Inmate Committee

In response to the demand of prisoners for a greater input
into the decision-making process, prisoner committees were
organized in Canadian prisons and procedures were implemented
for an ombudsman-type office to investigate complaints in the
corrections system. In Dorchester the inmate committee con-

sisted of elected representatives of the convicts who were to
present the views and interests of the prisoners to the prison
administration. In general, the committees tried to act as the
voice through which the prisoners could be heard, and they were
initially welcomed by the prisoners as an important reform.

In the early 1970s, coinciding with a large transfer of
inmates from Dorchester to Springhill, a large draft of prisoners were transferred east from the British Columbia penitentiary. These were described by prison staff as being more
sophisticated and a different type of prisoner than was found
in the Atlantic Provinces. In 1972, in the words of an official, several of these prisoners attempted to take over the
running of the prison by first capturing leading positions on
the Inmate Committee. These members became "power struck" (in
the jargon of the staff) and gave the administrators further
"headaches". Their demands were at times backed up by demonstrations of prisoners who refused to eat or to go to work.

As a result of a major disturbance in Dorchester, the
Inmate Committee was disbanded and, when the prison returned to
its usual condition, a new Inmate Committee was not constituted. Instead an Inmate Sports and Recreation Committee was
established, still with representatives of the prisoners elected from the cell blocks. Their sphere of activity, as the name
implies, was to organize recreation in the prison, thereby
expressing the devolution of decision-making from the unofficial representation of inmate grievances to the allotting of
some control over inconsequential matters. On an unofficial
basis the Recreation Committee represented individual prisoners
by bringing to the attention of the staff requests for TLAs or
transfers. It performed some of the functions of the Inmate
Committee although its terms of reference were changed. It had
no formal right to represent the prison population, and therefore merely raised issues with the staff on an individual
basis, leaving the initiative and the decision-making entirely
in the hands of the staff. The new Committee discussed mutual
problems in an informal atmosphere, as contrasted with the
overt atmosphere of antagonism prevalent during the period of
the real Inmate Committee in which the ideology which pitted
prisoners against the Administration legitimized the definition
of the Committee as representing the interests of the prisoners. The Inmate Committee had been instituted as a means to
ensure due process of complaints and grievances which would
leave the action in the hands of representatives. It was also
expected to bring potential problems to the attention of the
staff and serve as a means to calm things down. In practice,
the Inmate Committee had frequently heightened rebellion and
gave leadership to the tendency towards polarization. The
content of the demands depended on the objective conditions of
the prison and were reflected in specific election choices. In
the newer set-up, the administrative advantages of the weakened
Committee, which helped staff keep in touch with the mood of

the prisoners, was retained, while the political content involved in the representation of interests was eliminated.

An Inmate Committee was also formed in Springhill but it has also evolved through various forms over time. The Committee was formed of eight members, two representatives of each unit, and met twice a month. Over the period of its existence, from the administrative point of view, the representatives chosen varied from the best to the worst depending on the mood of the institution: when the conflicts were closer to the surface, "obnoxious" prisoners tended to be elected; otherwise "decent" prisoners got the nod. The TC apparently tended to elect "better" representatives.

The Committee's duties involved such things as organizing different projects, such as special family visit days, which were described as major events held twice a year. It was argued by staff members that the Committee served a rehabilitative function by placing inmates in a responsible position accountable for planning events. The Committee also functioned in a second way relating to the types of representatives: it gave the administration some indication of conflicts in the institution and thereby allowed steps to be taken to intervene, if possible, to influence the direction of events and control the situation in the prison. The Committee did not function as a grievance organization for prisoners. The grievance procedure was handled privately through senior administration and was not expected to arise in the Inmate Committee meetings. The staff was also left out of the discussion. The problems were brought directly to the top--if they were brought anywhere--and a disposition was provided after they are investigated. They were seen as individual problems rather than as individual manifestations of collective grievances. An Inmate Affairs Branch (of the Canadian Penitentiary Service) has been set up to deal with claims of individual prisoners which reach that higher stage.

In 1974 the guards came out strongly against the creation of Inmate Committees which, they argued, would potentially increase the use of strong-arm tactics among prisoners. They were supported by the Public Service Alliance of Canada in this stance. Thereupon, the Inmate Committees were temporarily disbanded and a Parliamentary Commission was established to investigate the situation. Later, Inmate Committees were re-established in some institutions but, again, without any real powers. According to the Sub-Committee on the Penitentiary System (1977), the rules of the game are such that the "Director has the power to remove any member of the Committee who does not adequately represent the inmates, is using his position on the Committee to the detriment of the inmates, or is using his position for his own personal purposes" (:99). Some maximums have still not had Inmate Committees restored. Those that have been reintroduced are of an ad hoc and precarious nature, acting more as a mechanism for keeping tabs on the prisoners.

The new reformism had attempted to liberalize the conditions of imprisonment. With a new generation of prisoners who were conscious of civil rights, the problem of maintaining traditional order intensified. There appeared to be a connection between the new reformism and the demonstrations, rebellions and hostage-taking incidents occurring with increasing frequency in Canadian prisons. One consequence of this was a further development of hostility and antagonism among custodial staff against both the prisoners and treatment officials in the prison.

In December 1974, five escapees from St. Vincent de Paul demanded press coverage of the conditions there, and cited guard brutality, the use of the "hole", drug use and homosexuality as some of the problems. The "hole" refers to a dissociation cell which serves as punishment for breaches of discipline. Punishment consists of solitary confinement on a restricted diet. The federal court in B. C. has ruled it "cruel and unusual treatment" (McCann vs. the Queen) but it has not been prohibited. Less than a year later, in response to the death on duty of an Archambault guard, 6500 prison guards walked off the job in a "day of protest" in an attempt to pressure the Cabinet to institute capital punishment. The RCMP and the Armed Forces patrolled the 49 penitentiaries and correctional centres (Enright 1977:32).

The Canadian Penitentiary Service responded to developments such as these with a combination of new legislation and some administrative changes. The government announced its intention to create a legislative package including gun control laws and changes which tightened bail and parole. Staff colleges were to offer training courses in crisis intervention and riot control. In the prisons, perimeter security was tightened and additional security officers were recruited. A Criminal Code Amendments Bill was introduced in the House of Commons which amended the areas of firearms control, electronic surveillance, the handling of dangerous offenders and the custody and release of inmates. A number of measures were introduced to attempt to reduce the access to guns by potentially dangerous people and police rights were to be expanded with respect to the use of electronic bugging systems. The legislation also proposed the imposition of an indeterminate sentence for all dangerous offenders, as well as measures designed to provide better control in penitentiaries. Statutory remission would be abolished, with only earned remission available. The maximum penalty for escape would be increased from five to ten years. The NPB would be expanded from nineteen to twenty-six members to ensure a more careful review of applicants.

In addition, reflecting the two-handed policy of the Cana-

dian government, the CPS announced a reform package which would
include better planned and smaller prisons, more rehabilita-
tions programmes and more Temporary Leaves of Absence. There
was considerable disagreement about these reforms. The Canadian Association of Police Chiefs protested that parole would
still be "too loose". Prison guards called rehabilitation a
costly waste; in the words of one, it was "a monumental farce
costing taxpayers millions of dollars" (Time 9 October 1974).
Media outcry over escapes and crimes committed on TLAs provoked
heavy criticism of penal reforms. There were cutbacks in the
number of paroles granted in the middle seventies because of
what was seen as an alarming number of parole violations. More
stringent screening procedures were applied and fewer applications were approved. Official viewpoints reflected a pessimism
about reform in pentitentiaries. William Outerbridge, Chairman
of the National Parole Board, said at the time that the "most
important single cause of the unrest, the dissatisfaction which
surrounds corrections today, is simply the fact that no consensus exists as to what the purposes of the system are and how
these aims can be achieved".

Meanwhile, prison after prison experienced major disturbances: Guelph, Maplehurst, Dorchester, Matsqui, New Westmin-
ster, Laval, Millhaven (Desroches 1983). After the 28 major
incidents in 1976, a Parliamentary Sub-committee was set up to
visit penitentiaries across Canada and to recommend solutions
to the problem of unrest in prisons. With talk of the failure
of the rehabilitative ethic even more widespread, a Gallup Poll
showed that 56 percent of Canadians thought that prisons were
"too soft" (Enright 1977:32). The report recommended a complete overhaul of the CPS, which was described as being exces-
sively bureaucratic: there were almost as many prison employ-
ees as prisoners. It also reported that management was not in
fact running the prisons, the directors having become "impotent
figureheads" as a result of the growth above them of the power
of regional offices, and below them in the hierarchy of command, of the power of the guards who were increasingly taking
decision-making into their own hands. From the guards point of
view, however, it is the prisoners who exercised control. At
best, they maintained the perimeters, fulfilling the function
of short-term protectors of civil society while watching over
an increasingly violent prison population (Taylor 1984). Partly as a result of this de facto dissociation, both murders and
suicides are endemic in Canadian prisons in the 1980s (Ross
1983). In Britain, industrial actions by guards have been
attributed to such factors as the rise in the prison population, the effect of the national prisoners' movement, the
increasing number of disturbances in the maximum prisons and
the general loss of confidence in the managers of the prison
system (King and Morgan 1980: vii).

The Principle of Confinement

The withdrawal of the guards from internal as opposed to perimeter control is indicative of the conservative response to the critique of the prison as an institution of reformation, and reflects the reiteration of what is viewed as its other main function: that is, that prison is a custodial institution and nothing more (Emery 1970:97). The more liberal-minded have not accepted the full implications of this stance. Hawkins, for example, settles for a view which posits a multiplicity of aims, related to the prisoner's classification. The top security risk category require only "control and confinement", a recommendation which is in accordance with a conservative emphasis. For other offenders, imprisonment serves no positive purpose and alternatives to imprisonment are suggested, from more general use of probation to expanded programmes of restitution and community service. He accepts the usual view of rehabilitation as individualized treatment, while more carefully delimiting the offenders at either end of the continuum who will not benefit from, or are not in need of, rehabilitation: "In between there will be many different categories of prisoners for whom a variety of different objectives, educational, vocational, disciplinary, remedial or therapeutic might feasibly be selected as primary" (Hawkins 1974:115). In other words, the traditional categories are maintained, although the number of offenders for whom rehabilitation is appropriate is diminished in theory, to correspond with the failure in practice.

The most interesting policy recommendation that comes from this view that, as Hawkins puts it, "the penitentiary system was, quite literally as it happens, a monumental mistake" (:115), is not the abolition of the prison, but the use of alternatives where feasible. On the contrary the prison is deemed necessary for those who are criminally engrained and who cannot be rehabilitated. From this perspective comes one significant recommendation: for "the development of much smaller, specialized custodial establishments designed to meet the diversity of our penal needs and purposes" (:115). This would include small maximum security institutions for high security risks in which the emphasis would be on control and confinement. In Canada a similar proposal suggested building a number of new mediums and maximums for 150 to 180 prisoners each over a five-year period. This was meant to ensure that there be no further Atticas--no large prison population in which politicization and collective action is readily feasible. In these small maximums the emphasis on security would mean little attempt to rehabilitate and the maximum use of coercion.

The loss of the diversity of the prison population might solidify the opposition of the prisoners, and the traditional problem of the 1950s prison, caused by the lack of a hierachy of rewards to complement the relatively narrow hierarchy of

126

punishments, would be reproduced. In such institutions, containing those defined as the most incorrigible, respressive measures would be more readily accepted by the general population if conditions precipitated rebellion. Acceptance of official brutality depends on the definition of the targets of this action as significantly different and evil. This is difficult to maintain with respect to the prison population as a whole--although this belief is a cornerstone of conservative penology--but super-maximums would more easily be seen by the public as reflecting a real difference which would justify the use of harsh measures. Officially, the prison administration remains wedded to a punitive model for all prisoners, and maintains that the prison is an appropriate means of punishment, not only for the criminal considered "engrained", but for others as well. The suggestion that the living unit programme be adopted in the maximums has not been implemented. Administrative reform in the maximum security prisons means the reorganization of staff (the "team principle", for example) as a means to make prison management more efficient. While the small maximums will supposedly have a more personal prisoner/counsellor relationship and better conditions, more importantly they would be easier to control: prison radicals could more easily be identified and isolated or transferred (Wright 1976:333).

If it is agreed that the majority of prisoners are not in need of institutional treatment, then this delegitimizes the use of hospital techniques for this group. But it legitimizes a more systematic use of such techniques on the minority of prisoners who are defined as being in need of it for their own good. Those who are defined as "borderline psychotic" in the jargon of administrative staff will be assigned to a new psychiatric prison and subjected to the potential use of mind-altering drugs, psycho-surgery, electric shock and the other modern paraphenalia of control in a mental hospital. The new prison could then be increasingly used as a scientifically sophisticated adjustment centre for those driven into irrationality by the wider society, but also for consciously rebellious prisoners deemed threatening.

A new control mechanism is in the area of drug use in prison--not primarily the nonmedical use of drugs by prisoners, but the putative medical prescription of drugs by the staff for use by the inmates. In addition to these measures of social control, there is the issue of the use of prisoners as experimental subjects by drug companies. In the United States a large proportion of prisoners volunteer to act as experimental subjects, and waive rights to sue for damages, in order to obtain money, perhaps to relieve boredom, and in the hopes of obtaining an earlier release. It has been estimated that 85 percent of the first human testing of newly developed drugs in the U.S. utilizes prisoner "volunteers". In the U. S. the National Commission for the Protection of Human Subjects of Biomedical and Behavioural Research has recommended that "nontherapeutic biomedical research" not be conducted in prisons. The use of pacification drugs to try to keep the prisoners in lines was not addressed, and by implication, it is left open.

The FCA and the Opportunities Principle

The new orthodoxy of the 1980s in Canada is to give the question of "rehabilitation" a back seat relative to a renewed emphasis on "sentence management". In 1974, the Solicitor General set up a task force to develop the role and organizational structure of a new Federal Corrections Agency (FCA) which would integrate the Penitentiary and Parole Services. This task force consulted with staff at all levels, representatives of private and after-care agencies, police, provincial correctional agencies, as well as some guards and inmates. A sub-task force was to prepare an inventory and analysis of all programmes carried out by both services and a review of the programme planning process in a number of programmes. It would also have to come up with a proposed programme planning model.

The official response to the talk about the failure of "rehabilitation" came out in the statement from the Solicitor General on the role of Federal Corrections in Canada (Task Force 1977). This report reviewed the state of corrections in the late 1970s which were "experiencing rapid and complex change that, coupled with a dramatic increase in the incidence of violence, has pushed us into the spotlight of public scrutiny and has left correctional staff without a clear sense of direction". In this situation, "assumptions have been challenged and correctional administrators have undergone soul-searching reexaminations of their own correctional goals and objectives" (:iv-v). In the Task Force's view, federal correction's should be based on humane treatment while administering the sentence imposed by the court. Policies about corrections should not be determined solely by public opinion, although public acceptance and support are important. Correctional agencies must provide leadership rather than follow broad social trends. In this respect, the correctional service was setting itself up as more liberal than the Canadian population. The report mentions public concern over the many disturbances in prisons and how, more than ever, public safety and accountability will have to be a primary concern. However, rather than abandon the idea of community corrections, the Task Force recommended revisions, including a demand for a greater role in the development of correctional policy by the private sector. Increasing cooperation between federal and provincial correctional agencies in policy development was also advocated. A National Advisory Network was established to serve as a coordinating body for federal-provincial endeavours, responsible for the development and implementation of innovative models, and correctional manpower training and development.

In retrospect, the guiding philosophy of corrections pro-

posed by the Task Force reiterateed the need for a more unified
administration of criminal justice, a never-ending litany of
previous Royal Commissions and Task Forces. From the point of
view of the philosophy of rehabilitation, however, the task
force rejected the model as it had been defined up to that
time: that the responsibility for the success or failure to
rehabilitate the offender rested with the correctional agencies
rather than with the individual concerned. If criminal behaviour is a manifestiation of a deep personality disorder,
then rehabilitation not only requires extensive treatment,
which is an unrealistic goal for penitentiaries, but also
requires a committment from the offender. It was primarily
misconceptions about this latter aspect of rehabilitation which
had led to the public placing the blame for failure on the
correctional authorities. The Task Force, however, did not
advocate returning to a strict punishment model. It agrgued
that the failure of the correctional system to recognize the
responsibility of the offender had led to the abuse of authority under the medical model. This model, which formed the basis
of the rehabilitative ideal, wrongly minimized offenders' responsibility for their crimes by assuming they were sick for
reasons not of their making. This "approach gives correctional
practitioners a strong inducement to employ coercion in the
guise of human treatment, and enforces participation in treatment programmes as a requisite to release" (:27), a situation
which results in distrust among offenders and an undermining of
treatment goals.

Another problem with the rehabilitative approach was seen
to be its emphasis on expertise for solving problems. This was
harmful, the Task Force declared, because it relieved the
community of its responsibility in corrections. The fact that
the task force argued that unrealistic expectations had been
generated did not mean, in its view, an admission of failure or
a "copping out" on the part of Federal Corrections. It merely
reflected an unrealistic approach to corrections which ignored
certain basic principles. The main revision suggested was the
explicit adoption of the "opportunities principle". Federal
Corrections was still charged with providing correctional opportunities "designed to assist the offender in the development
of daily living skills, confidence to cope with his personal
problems and social environment and the capacity to adopt more
acceptable conduct norms." The opportunities principle, however, was "based on the assumption that the offender is ultimately responsible for his behaviour....The offender is convicted and sentenced on the basis of his criminal behaviour,
not on the basis of some underlying personality disorder or
deprived socio-economic condition" (:30-31). It was the role
of the courts to establish guilt or innocence and the role of
corrections to manage the sentence imposed by the court. The
Task Force softened its line on individual responsibility by
discussing the shared responsibility of correctional staff,
offender and community in the correctional process. Although

the offender was ultimately responsible for his or her criminal behaviour, the community was also responsible for providing opportunities for law-abiding behaviour. The role of Federal Corrections was to manage the sentence and provide treatment opportunities, while the inmate, with the help of professional guidance, was to select the appropriate programme. A further recommendation called for the development of mechanisms to channel prisoner grievances and protect prisoner rights.

The Solicitor General of Canada announced that the reha- bilitation model would be replaced in the 1980s by an "opportu- nities-incentive model" (Cousineau and Plecas 1982: 309). Cor- rectional officials were quick to adopt this new justification. In Springhill it was denied by senior staff members that rehabilitation, as a philosophy, had ever existed, and that the opportunities principle more accurately described exactly what had always been done. Upon being admitted to the institution, the prisoner had been informed of what facilities were available in the prison; he was reminded of the maximum and minimum lengths of his incarceration, and the conclusion was drawn that what use the prisoner made of the facilities over time depended entirely on him. There were concrete incentives, such as earlier parole, attached to the participation in pro- grammes, for which the prisoner must apply. The prisoner similarly had a choice of working or not working, with the understanding that to choose noncompliance would mean a period in isolation (dissocation). In addition, there were other incentives such as prison pay (which is low, but pressure has been mounted to increase it), temporary leaves, and so on. The basic point was that the responsibility of the prison system was to provide opportunities and inducements of an appropriate kind, but that ultimately the responsibility for reformation rested on the individual incarcerated.

This standard retrospective denial of the rehabilitation philosophy begs the question. There was always a distinction between the rehabilitative programmes devised and the motiva- tion of prisoners to participate. By definition if the prisoner did not take the programme seriously, then no rehabil- itation benefits could result; but it has been assumed that if the prisoner did actively fulfil his role in the programme (e.g. take vocational training seriously) then he could be rehabilitated. The opportunities principle does not negate rehabilitation--it more precisely defines it to take the re- sponsibility for failure away from the prison, while leaving responsibility for success at least partly with the staff and programmes. This rejection of rehabilitation means that the prisoner is not to be regarded as sick, which is seen as the intrusion of moral labeling and condemnation. The sick ap- proach, carried out to its logical extent, implied that the prisoner was not responsible for his actions. Now it is merely held that prisoners have troubled personalities but they are responsible for their actions. So the staff can still justify

the use of therapy but they do not have to feel guilty about
its failure.

The New Behaviourism

In contrast to an impressionistic social work format of
the old medical model and rehabilitation, the Canadian Penitentiary System has attempted to adopt a more rigorous image.
Requests for new programmes or justifications to the Treasury
Board for the continuation of old ones have to be couched in
scientific terminology with statistical data. The key concepts
are programme planning and sentence management. Sentence management is not so much opposed to rehabilitation, it is argued,
but rather is a component of it, and in each case it involves
four considerations: the protection of the society, the welfare of the offender, retributive punishment, (reintroduced as
a theoretically important element) and mutual agreement on
individual programme planning.

One of the origins of the last item, the development of an
individual's programme participation, had its origins in the
classification movement and has been most explicitly implemented in the United States. In some jurisdictions it consists
of a legal contract between the prisoner and the authorities
(presumably binding, although it might be argued that it is
signed under duress). The prisoner agrees to be responsible to
do certain things which are as fully spelled out in behavioural
objectives and as capable of objective assessment as possible.
For example, it is agreed that the inmate will complete a
specific training programme following a declared routine by a
stated date, to be on "good behaviour" (also spelled out as
"objectively" as possible), and so on. The responsibility of
the authorities lies in their agreement to provide the facilities for training. In the United States, the Mutual Agreement
Program is legally binding, and contract violations can be
taken to court through a litigation process. The Canadian
recommendation, Individual Program Planning, included a non-
legally binding contract; it was an agreement only. The courts
would not be involved and the prisoners could not sue for the
prison's failure to live up to the contract. In place of the
old rehabilitation there is diagnostic interviewing, which is
merely a redefinition of the medical model with the crucial
additional component that it attempts to be unambiguous about
the prisoner's responsibility and the resulting legitimacy of
punishment. In the interview, needs are assessed and a programme is devised in an atmosphere of recrimination with the
responsibility solely on the shoulders of the condemned individual.

The staff, having abandoned the concept of rehabilitation,
no longer needs to defend it. Even their best effort may be to
no avail in trying to change the criminally incorrigible. The
"unworkable", "unmotivate", "hostile" prisoner is simply as-

signed to control--sentence management is merely retribution,
"humane control" and public protection. He had been given the
opportunity to contract with the authorities but had not, and
is responsible for his condition. Recidivists similarly had
failed to live up to the agreement, having not "gone straight"
upon release. The staff no longer has to defend the image of
the rehabilitator. The law and order perspective prescribes
that prisoners are a dangerous and difficult lot, and the staff
agrees that it is virtually impossible to change them. They
can manage them in the sense that they can see to it that the
commitments are kept--for example, by ensuring that prisoners
do not escape custody and thereby escape part of their retributive punishment. Crime is defined as a community problem,
society's problem, everyone's problem equally. Since the generation of crime and criminals is in social processes usually
of a relatively undefined nature, then it is unrealistic to
achieve individual solutions to crime. Some intervention in
criminal careers may be successful, but prison and parole staff
are responsible at best for trying to control these problems
and cannot realistically cure them. In this fashion the
liberal social worker comes to cynical terms with his job.

This philosophy is spread through staff training sessions.
Courses for staff include dealing with hostage-taking incidents
and office occupations. Staff training and development programmes become a fringe benefit of employment, with travel
grants to distant conferences and sessions. The upshot of all
this is that the staff is becoming specialized. A new facility
for staff training has been opened at Memramcook. If such a
facility had operated in the late 1960s or early 1970s, we can
speculate that it would have stressed counselling and training
which were consistent with the rehabilitative ideal. The new
national priority--as in the case of the staff of the CCC--is
to train personnel in management and supervisory skills. The
claim is that there are enough social scientists and social
workers in the field but people in management positions often
know nothing about management or budgets. The priority of the
institution, which was designed originally to train security
officers, is now to train people to more effectively "run the
business".

The recent plethora of legislative changes and proposals
have been presented as reforms. In substance, the chief
characteristics of the proposed changes amount to a reiteration
of the prison as a place of confinement and punishment, while
certain measures, such as the new inmate committee, are added
to conjure up a progressive image. In contrast to the reformism which tried unsuccessfully to transform the prison from a
lock-up to a centre for rehabilitation, the new "reforms" are
based on the premise of punishment. In short, prison reform
means the expansion and consolidation of the hierachy of
punishment.

CHAPTER TEN

CONCLUSION

Since the passing of the Great American Celebration, western social science has been in considerable disarray. The predominance of structural functional analysis, which was undergirded by post-war material prosperity, has been broken. The development of historical experience exposed in practice what the radical critics had understood in theory: functionalism universalized a temporary period of social stability in advanced western nations into a "grand" theoretical justification. Despite some marginal criticism, the ideological root of "end of ideology" thinking was not fully exposed until, as a theoretical mode, it failed to account for changing historical experience.

In the place of a relatively established theory, a myriad of seemingly different models or "paradigms", developed by those Reasons calls "paradigm entrepreneurs" (1974), compete for ideological hegemony. The analysis of social theory in the realm of penology and criminology indicates that this situation is not without precedent, but it also shows that there have been periods in the past when dominant ideologies held sway for considerable periods. Nevertheless, this area as well is currently undergoing a process of ideological turmoil and it is this process of change and its programmatic consequences which have been our primary focus. While change has been incessant and periodic in correctional ideology, it is remarkable how stable certain traditional outlooks have been in the correction field. The changes in penology which have been analzed--with the possible exception of the transition from a general metaphysical conception to the classical model--can hardly be termed revolutions. More importantly, even with respect to this particular transition, the main question has not been the supersession of one paradigm over another but the incorporation of substantial ideological elements from the old in the new. From this vantage point they seem to have more in common with a theory of epicycles than with revolutions.

Individualization of Treatment

We have seen that the classical emphasis on rationally determining the amount of punishment according to the severity of the breach of law, was modified by the recognition that abstractly equal sanctions are not, in fact, equal. The resulting neo-classical modifications are usually interpreted as the first important steps in the individualization of "correction" (Cressey 1972: 440-441). With the rise of a rehabilitative philosophy, the old view suggesting that penalties were to be determined by the type of infraction has been modified by

134

notions that, in individual cases, the consolidated behaviour
pattern of the individual, as well as the peculiar circumstances surrounding the act, should be taken into consideration in
the sentencing process (Glaser 1972).

The mechanical positivists of the nineteenth century also
contributed to the individualization of punishment. Gall, the
father of phrenoloy, who posited a physical relation between
criminality and brain structure, also stressed the need for
individualized punishment (Sellin 1972). Sellin has traced the
concept of individual treatment to the "moral insanity" viewpoint of Benjamin Rush and his followers who concluded that
criminality was a form of "mental illness", and therefore ought
to be "treated" rather than "punished". With this background,
the contemporary philosophy of rehabilitation pushes the individualization to the farthest point, in one-to-one counselling.
The social causation thesis is acknowledged as having produced
psychological shortcomings in individuals; but individual processes are deemed capable of rectifying the initial errors.

The rise historically of a reform ideology in Canada was
intimately connected with an ethos of Christian morality and
temperance which was solidly rooted in religious views which
maintained a metaphysical distinction between good and bad
people. The reformers, largely middle class "humanitarians",
defined as a social responsiblity the "care, protection and
improvement of defectives, dependents and delinquents", the
latter broadly including "the careless, the spendthrift, the
improvident, the shiftless, the drunkard and the criminal"
(Daires 1903: 341), all of whom were moral defectives. The
three goals outlined for these individuals who occupied space
at the fringes of society were: "care, protection and improvement" In the case of criminals in particular, the "protection"
referred above all to the protection of the law-abiding public.

While these deplorable individual characteristics were at
first thought of as ultimately deriving from an essentially
flawed and unchanging "human nature", the rapid industrialization occurring about the turn of the century in major Canadian
centres enormously exacerbated social problems and gave rise
subsequently not only to an active and conscious reform element
with some practical social policy connotations, but also gave
an important impetus to the rise of sociological consciousness.
In the realm of social theories there was some understanding
that individual character itself was at least in part socially
formed, and that "while many are responsible themselves for
their condition...countless thousands are not"(Daires 1903).

It was this distinction which was of crucial significance.
The development of positive criminology, in both its natural-
istic and its social forms, tended to undermine the arguments
supporting the notion of individual responsibility for criminal
action, and therefore ultimately led to the rejection of retri-

butive punishment. In subsequent ideological developments, the
crucial issue had been to somehow reconcile the classical and
positive notions into some reasonable compromise in which individual responsibility was retained but some social responsibility was accepted. Consequently, the penal system incorporated some attention to "improvement" as well as "punishment". The distinction was drawn between "the reformable and
the incorrigible".

The most important debate within penology has been between
the conservative emphasis on incorrigibility, retributive punishment, and an extreme separation between the criminal and the
non-criminal, and the liberal emphasis on individual reform of
those amenable to change, institutional reform for more "humane" confinement, and a more flexible separation between the
criminal and the noncriminal. Until recently the liberal expectation had been that the goal of individual reformation was
realizable within the prison, that it was compatible with the
degree of punishment consistent with imprisonment. If the
prison experience itself did not change prisoners in the appropriate direction then at least programmes could be devised
within the walls to facilitate the process. Reform, then,
comprised two aspects: the physical change of the prison (for
example, the differentiation of types of prisons and changes in
architecture), and the development of increasingly innovative
programs designed to change individuals.

Within positivist theory there was the the possibility of
distinguishing between actual social problems and the individual manifestation of these problems, and several varieties of
social causation were posited. In addition, an element of
social, institutional reform was introduced and progressivists
postulated that social problems could eventually be solved in a
piecemeal fashion. The process of reform was necessarily two-
fold: a general objective reform of social condition and an
individual reformation of those who had suffered through the
inequalities and injustices of the given social environment.
It was ludicrous to reform an individual and return him to the
same situation from which his criminal action originated. The
social view of the world, then, promised much in the way of
change.

As corrections evolved, however, the progressive social
element withered and was subject to a continuing process of
individualization whch tended to reduce social problems to the
level of the individual. The conflict between the liberal view
of progressive change and the conservative emphasis on imposing
the assumed social consensus on individual deviants was resolved by increasing the emphasis on changing individual attitudes and skills and redefining institutional reform narrowly
to mean manipulating social arrangements in the prison to
facilitate this individual transformation. The philosophy of
rehabilitation justified the attempt to transform individuals

in ways deemed desirable based on the view that manipulating individual charateristics and motivations rather than changing concrete social reality was the appropriate response to problems.

The most significant ideological expression of this reforming trend was the medical model of rehabilitation which stressed the possibility and desirability of individual reformation based on a process of intervention in the prisoners' psyches to overcome specific deficiencies which were assumed causally related wih criminaltiy. But there was not a sense in which rehabilitation replaced the classical punitive model but rather was grafted onto it. The rehabilitators came into the prison and supplemented the custodial/punitive staff. Despite its predominance in academic circles, the view that the prison is for rehabilitation and not for punishment has reflected a minority view within the field of practical penology.

Nevertheless, the list of reforms devised during the period of rehabilitation is lengthy and would include vocational and educational training in the prison, recreational activities, psychological counselling, medium and minimum prisons, therapeutic communities, living units, prison "camps", community correctional and residential centres, TLAs, day-paroles, drug treatment centres--and a number of others. Many of these resulted from studies commissioned by the government which reported conditions to be virtually unchanged from previous studies and recommended solutions which were given some concrete implementation. But with the exception of parole, which is hardly a new concept, and CRCs, which merely provide temporary "bed and breakfast" type accommodation, the reforms eventually reach only a minority of prisoners, and therefore do not even begin to meet the needs identified in the initial reports. And, in the meantime, the maximum prisons remain deplorable and the minimums become increasingly like maximums. The social optimism which buoyed up hopes and was based upon the then solid foundation of an expanding economy which could be funnelled into reformist channels had dried up in a period of austerity and cutbacks, and the rehabilitative philosophy was attacked as one of the frills which had to go.

The development of the reform philosophy and its implementation was generally the result of specific crises in the prison system which were brought to the attention of the public by the actions of the prisoners themselves. The failure of rehabilitation is not merely its failure to produce noncriminals from criminals but, more fundamentally, its failure to maintain control. This is not to assert that institutions have some internal dynamics of their own which lead to the preservation of established routines, but to place the prison in the social context as being an institution of coercion necessary for the power of the state--which is preserved by both repressive measures and specific kinds of reformist ones.

There has, however, been a differing emphasis from time to
time on one or other of these mechanisms. The traditional
punitive approach has generally been ineffective in promoting
long term stability, a conclusion which means that social
control must also entail a development of an alternative r-
eformist strategy (related to the degree of availability of
adequate social resources). The degree of commitment to the
rehabilitative ideal has been called into question with reference to trends in expenditure for the policy relative to those
earmarked for "corrections". In 1962-3, 34.72 percent of the
federal and provincial funds for administering criminal justice
in Canada went into "correction" and 48.55 percent to the
police. Despite the proclamation of the years of rehabilitation, in 1971-72 the proportion had changed to 29.41 percent
for corrections and 55.24 percent for police, and, if local
government expenditures, are included the amount spent on the
police increases to nearly 70 percent (Department of Solicitor
General 1978: 20-28. The proportion spent on "corrections" is
allocated between security and rehabilitation and some shifts
in this occurred with the hiring of trained rehabilitative
staff. But this trend has also been reversed and more money is
being spent on expanding the security staff and increasing
their remuneration. What the figures show is that, regardless
of the reform philosophy, correctional authorities remain wedded to coercive control.

The model of the rehabilitated prisoner, or the prisoner
successfully responding to the prison programmes, assumed that
the prison was operating in the interests of the prisoner. The
fact that the "reformed" prisoner was also a "model" prisoner
in the eyes of the prison administration was acknowledged as
self-evident. As implemented, the philosophy of rehabilitation
attempted to convince prisoners that the problem of criminality
was within themselves, that the prison was designed to help
them and that they were in need of a specific kind of attitude
change. The intervention of treatment programmes must first of
all undercut the tendency to develop anti-administrative attitudes, the naturally developing arising conflict consciousness
(which is reinforced by some aspects of the prison "culture"),
and replace them with "trust". This is based on the actual
contradiction between the objective collective interests of
prisoners and the structured reward system which counter-poses
individual interests.

One standard viewpoint in criminology has been to assert
that the goals of imprisonment are contradictory, consequently,
that they work at cross purposes, and hence it is no wonder
that rehabilitation procedures do not work (Gibbons 1977: 12-
13). Essentially the conflict of goals is between a punitive
response and a rehabilitative response, and it is assumed that
there is a zero-sum relationship between the two such that an
increase in the punitive aspect must produce a proportional
decrease in the treatment aspect. For example, allocation of

scarce financial resources is divided between increased measures for security--the attempt to obtain internal order by coercion--and programmes designed to inculate positive values. In Gibbons' view, "the present schizoid character of the sum of reactions to deviants poses severe obstacles to efforts to change law-breakers into conforming citizens"(1977: 13).

The prison situation, at its most simplistic, places two groups of people in a situation of coercion based on unequal power, such that the objective interests of the two are contradictory. Drawn to its logical conclusion, this would suggest the tendency to develop a consciousness of opposition among prisoners which in a social context can become solidaristic. There are numerous cross-cutting features which derive from the nature of the society, the characteristics of the prison as it is institutionalized, as well as from conscious manipulation on the part of prison administrators, treatment staff and professional social scientists, which operate in the opposite direction and serve to undercut the development of solidary opposition.

The conservative and liberal standpoints assert the primacy of either one or the other aspect--punishment or treatment; the crucial point, however, is that the object of the process is the same, and the conflict is merely over the appropriate balance of punishment and reward, for the "protection of society" demands prisons. According to the populist right-wing view, this is so because there are in our midst "criminals"--an absolute category which can be contrasted with "conforming citizens"--and the former must be isolated from the latter and transformed into law-abiding people where possible. Obviously the real situation is far more complicated than this. The retort that victimizers are also social victims is only true to a degree; in some respects dominant and privileged groups are the chief victimizers.

While the usual arguments against increasing the punitiveness of the prisons are based on "humanitarian" objections, there is also among criminologists the view that negative sanctions alone produce unintended consequences; in particular, that harsh conditions produce rebellion. It is not only that the emphasis on the punitive justification for imprisonment hinders the opportunities for rehabilitation, although this is an argument which is frequently raised. The argument that prison is a crucible of crime rests in part on the reactions to punishment itself. Consequently, an increase in punitive measures would lead to an subsequent increase in the failure rate. The conservative viewpoint has drawn the opposite conclusion: the curtailment of punishment implied by the rehabilitative programmes prevents the prison from adequately fulfilling its deterrent function. Rehabilitation and punishment, then, are seen as antithetical goals, and the emphasis on one of these aspects is automatically linked with a de-emphasis on the other.

This conceptual separation of these two goals, and the view that one aspect suffers at the expense of the other, was further complicated by the development of a dual staff, one sector of which was defined as "security" and was responsible for enforcing the deprivations of prison life and preventing any diminution of the punitive aspect, and a second sector, the "treatment staff", who were responsible for the rehabilitation of the prisoner. Positive alternatives were expected to diminish the deprivations of incarceration and thereby increase the motivation for compliance, with motivation being seen mechanically as a reognition that certain ends can be achieved by certain actions. In many respects this separation is no longer regarded in the same way as it had been in Canada in the 1960s or in the United Stats in the 1950s. The treatment staff in many of the modern correctional programmes performs both coercive and treatment functions becoming more overtly responsible for social control. This is institutionalized to a degree in the opportunities priniciple under which the staff has become mere "people managers".

One of the key theoretical critiques of radical criminology is that both punitive and reform aspects serve the same function: the maintenance of social control in the society. Beyond this simple formula are two important facts: first, the two strategies are not equal and social order is ultimately founded on the threat and practice of violence. Second, the utilization of reform as a means of control is limited by several factors. The most significant is the absolute aggregate of public funds which are available for the implementation of reform proposals. The systematic introduction of the philosophy of rehabilitation occurred during the post-war years when, despite some relatively minor recessions and a consistent if rather small annual rate of inflation, welfare state interventions seemed to have produced long term stability. The failure of rehabilitation in the late-1970s and early 1980s is associated with stagflation and the unprecedented form of the economic crisis. There is some foundation in fact for the view that the philosophy of rehabilitation had never been given an adequate chance in terms of resources, but this must be understood first in relation to the aggregate of resources possible and to the priority of expenditure. To exaggerate the point, if every criminal had a full time social worker with sufficient resources to meet elementary needs for a decent life for the criminal and his family then recidivism may quite conceivably decline. What seems possible in theory is not always possible when the concrete circumstances are taken into account.

A further point is that there is a limit to the extent to which the aggregate social resources devoted to "corrections" can be distributed to the treatment end of the continuum of control. This is so primarily because the basis of the state's maintenance of social order is to be found in its control over the organization of social violence, with the prison acting as an important institutionalized expression of this control. Recourse to the means of violence proceeds by way of a hierachy of responses and over time the level of resources diverted to the function of coercive control can vary. The relative emphasis on one aspect or the other within the given allocation of resources is dependent upon the degree of social threat perceived by the state, a perception which is not based solely on criminal statistics, but reflects other forms of social dissent. The locus of the increase in coercive control is not specific to one institution but is generalized and the "law and order" philosophy is reactivated in the sphere of policing and criminal justice as well as corrections. The new orientation is presented as a "reform" which, in Canada, usually contains some elements of a positive approach; in such periods, however, its characteristic is predominantly punitive.

The perspective of the custodians, who tend to adopt the clearly metaphysical separation of good and evil people, with prisoners defined to fall within the latter, simply asserts that the best way to maintain control is through segregation and systematic rules. The problem with this--clearly recognized by the early penologists--is that these measures are most effective when they are supplemented by possible inducements. That is, relative to staying locked in the cell for 24 hours, to be locked in the segregation compound, euphemistically called in contemporary jargon an "adjustment centre, does not represent a very significant escalation of punishment.

At the present impasse in corrections, almost all but a small band of reformers now accept the fact that prison reform in its various historic and recent manifestations has failed. Even the recent most provocative attempts to include inmates collectively in their own reformation have come to nought. Reforms implemented within the liberal ideology, or the apparently more radical, one eventually come to rest on the simple pole of individual rehabilitation in the context of repressive control. The fundamental feature of the prison--its punitive quality--always comes back to haunt the reformer. The law and order ideology of retribution wreaked against malevolence waits in the wings when the inexorable logic of prison experience brings too much rebellion to the centre stage. If prison must punish and, if all else seems to fail, then traditional methods maintain the most consistent aura of truth and straightforwardness.

The Future of Reform

Our analysis of the ideological and social meaning of prison reform results in a highly critical response to corrections as commonly conceived. The concept of prison reform has two potentially opposing aspects. If reform means simply to

141

attempt to alter the behaviour of a certain portion of the
population toward acceptable standards, then literaly everyone,
even prison inmates, involved in the correctional endeavour
conceives that reform is necessary. The most radical response
by prisoners and by criminology has been to question the standards of behaviour required, or, more precisely, the whole
value system of contemporary society, and the manner by which
such change of the value system should take place. On the
other side, the thrust of corrections as traditionally perceived does not accept this questioning of the whole mode of
societal organization. It is here where both the liberal
reformers with their emphases on individual rehabilitation and
the conservative retributionists with their emphasis on punishment actually meet in one convergent body of assumptions. This
convergence is based on agreeement on two fundamentals postulates.

The first is a separation between the healthy society and
the unhealthy or criminogenic parts of it. Whether criminality
is seen as rooted in essential human nature, in biological/
medical causes, or social factors, conservatives and liberals
agree that there are criminals in our healthy midst and something must be done to either quarantine the danger or to transform the danger into something as healthy as the rest of society. Even the attempt to conceive criminal behaviour as sick
behaviour and treat it psychiatrically or medically does not
alter this picture. To try to change a criminal into a patient
is only an indication of social hypocrisy since criminal
behaviour still retains its traditional aura and its definition
as a menace to an essentially healthy social fabric.

The second basic postulate common to both liberal reform
and conservative retribution is the acceptance of an externally
imposed authority system to operate the instruments of correction. While the reformer stresses the role of the rehabilitator or therapeutic professional and the traditionalist stresses
the role of the custodian and sometimes the knout, they both
agree that people other than the inmates themselves must decide
on the treatment appropriate to supposedly alter behaviour. As
we have indicated in our case study of the therapeutic community, rehabilitative attempts to include inmates in the decision-
making process remain cooptative and manipulative as long as
ultimate power resides in the prison authority system. Thus,
even the most innovative programmes attempting to increase
inmate participation must be seen as a continuation of the
prison control process.

It is the convergence of these two assumptions in the
context of prison being an essentially delimiting and repres-
sing institution which transforms the reformer, who accepts
theories of individual rehabilitation, into just another instrument for the control of prisoners. Wider social and economic causes may generate swings between law and order in the

prison and the individual rehabilitation of inmates, but they remain two sides of the same ideological coin as long as the basic social structure remains intact.

The fundamental limitation of all preexisting prison reform has been the assumption that such reform can take place disconnected from reform of the larger society. The prison is a place which confines and physically controls excessive social failures in a society whose central evaluative thrust must generate social failure. Those in prison come from the most restricting social environments which propel them into specific kinds of crimes against property, giving them the least protection against getting caught, convicted and sentenced to prison. The contemporary social system nurtures competitive individualism in the context of material scarcity (real and induced). The great value put on material acquisition in this context means that a very few people attain social success. The few successful through their control of the ideological apparatus define the legal system as one which protects their social positions. Moreover, their power gives them rights to avoid being defined as criminal for greater infractions of the legal system than the social failures who get caught and incarcerated for lesser crimes of the same type.

"Property is theft" said the 19th century social critic, Proudhon, and, in a society which sanctifies the accumulation of property, the biggest property owners may be the biggest thieves. The line between legal acquisition and illegal acquisition of property becomes blurred, the only difference being the amount of power which legal property musters both to define its property as legitimate and to avoid criminal proceedings when it breaks the law. That there is a great deal of property crime committed in large economic enterprise is documented in the now classic White Collar Crime by E. H. Sutherland (1949). The bigger the economic power, the bigger the potential crime and the greater the potential to get away with it.

Crimes against property then are the most common forms of crime and they are built into the normal functioning of Canadian society. They are so normal that the number of crimes actually occurring are much less than the number either reported or discovered. Moreover, the process of catching and convicting a perpetrator of this or any other type of crime funnels out those people of higher social and economic position and leaves only the most powerless to face a prison sentence. Bertrand Russell, the British philosopher, after entering prison for pacifist activities during World War I, remarked facetiously that he found his fellow inmates little different morally from the rest of humankind, the only difference being that they had been caught.

Prison, then, is a place for the already defeated in a society which glorifies victory and assures that very few will

have the opportunity to legally accumulate goods. Societal
claims to free choice for all are belied by the institutional
control of the marketplace by the economically powerful few.
It is no surprise that those who have no legitimate opportunity
to have what everyone is taught to want will use whatever means
at hand to get it. |The people with least opportunity are the
ones who are most likely to get caught and imprisoned for acts
that everyone else is committing.| The truth of this observa-
tion is humorously borne out in university classes in Social
Problems or Criminology where young students of predominantly
middle-class background discover, under questioning, that
literally all of them have already committed offenses of a
criminal nature.

To think that locking away criminals is getting rid of
crime in our kind of society is one of the central illusions of
the correctional system. | The average cynicism of the average
prison inmate is bred not only by prison experience alone, but
also by his recognition, if only implicit, that he lives in a
dog-eat-dog world, the only difference between himself and
others being the fact that he has been caught doing the biting.
To think that prison gives new alternatives for "going
straight" is only adding further degradation to the process.
William Outerbridge, Chairman of the National Parole Board,
acknowledged the irony of the prison when he observed that the
"obscenity" of prison arises from the contradiction that a
criminal is assumed to "make choices and, out of all the available alternatives, chose to commit an offense. When we put him
in prison, we take away every opportunity of choice he has and
then we expect him to be able to make the right choices after
he's been released"(Enright 1977).

In an opportunity system which has already been rigged
against those social types who happen to be in prison, the
inmate cannot be presented with a wider and more varied body of
social possibilities than the proverbial man on the street.
This seems to us the reason why the use of prison labour has
always been marginal to rehabilitative ideology, at best, hol-
low make-work and, at worst, the chain gang. The return to a
more punitive prison model may even lead to a greater exploitation of inmates as budget cutbacks generate demands for prisoners to do something to pay for their confinement. Real productive labour with adequate material rewards is impossible in
this kind of society, since it would completely undermine the
incentive to work outside prison, and the development of useful
products in prison would compete with the output of established
economic enterprise.

In critically evaluating crime and the correctional
system, we are in no way suggesting that crime makes no difference or that prisons should be all done away with immediately as has been suggested by some seemingly highly radical
criminologists. Not all prison reform falls into the category

144

of individual rehabilitation administered by external agents of
societal authority. Many of the demands made by solidary
prisoner groups connect prison reform to the wider demands of
societal transformation. And they do not reject the idea that
prisons may be necessary even in a transformed society, especially for some of the present inmates, or some not yet
imprisoned, who everyone can agree are too dangerous to be on
the loose. But they do see the prison in the present societal
context, whether punitive or rehabilitative, as a more excessive injustice in an inherently unjust society.

Up to now, individual rehabilitation has proceeded in
isolation from general institutional change in the rest of
society, a fact which accounts for its illusory character.
Since behaviour, attitudes and social response in general are
shaped by environmental influences, to be de-incarcerated to an
unchanged (in fact often worsened) family, work, and social
situation virtually necessitates the resumption of previous
modes of conduct (even assuming they have changed in prison).
The socio-economic circumstances of the offender, coupled with
the stigma which accrues to imprisonment, throw into sharp
relief the discrepancy between individual "reformation" and the
social situation which generates crime and the present prison
system. Only a change in socio-economic circumstances, a
change which may see inmates as part of a wide political movement, will ultimately affect the ideology and organization of
corrections.

REFERENCES

Allen, Harry E. and Clifford E. Simorsen
    1975 Corrections in America: An Introduction. London:
          Collier Macmillan.

American Correctional Association
    1966 Manual of Correctional Standards. Washington, D.C.
          American Correctional Association.

American Correctional Association
    1972 Report of the American Prison Association's
          Committee on Riots. Washington, D.C.

American Freinds Service Committee
    1971 Struggle for Justice: A Report on Crime and
          Punishment in America. N.Y. Hill and Wang.

Arboleda-Florez, J.
    1983 "The ethics of psychiatry in prison society",
          Canadian Journal of Criminology, Vol. 25, No. 1
          (January): 147-154.

Archambault Commission
    1939 Report of the Royal Commission to Investigate the
          Penal System of Canada. (Ottawa: King's Printer).

Bailey, Walter C.
    1966 "Correctional outcomes: An evaluation of 100
          reports", Journal of Criminal Law, Criminology and
          Police Science, Vol. 57 No. 2: 153-160.

Barlow, D. (Ed.)
    1971 A Review of Selected Criminological Research on
          the Effectiveness of Punishments and Treatments.
          Toronto: University Press.

Barnes, Harry Elmer
    1972 The Story of Punishment: A Record of Man's
          Inhumanity to Man. Montclair, N.J.: Patterson Smith.

Barnes, Harry Elmer and N. K. Teeters
    1951 New Horizons in Criminology. (2nd Ed.) New York:
          Prentice Hall.

Bean, Philip
    1976 Rehabilitation and Deviance. London: Routledge and
          Kegan Paul.

Becker, G.
1968   "Crime and punishment: An economic approach",
       Journal of Political Economy, LXXVI.

Becker H.
1963   Outsiders: Studies in the Sociology of Deviance.
       Glencoe, Ill.: Free Press.

Becker, H.
1967   "Whose side are we on?" Social Problems, XIV: 239-
       247.

Beech, C. E. and A. I. Gregerson
1964   "Three-year follow-up study: Drug addiction
       clinic", Canadian Journal of Corrections, Vol. VI, No.
       2: 211-224.

Bishop, Norman
1974   "Aspects of European prison systems". Pp. 83-100 in
       L. Blom-Cooper (Ed.) Progress in Penal Reform. Oxford:
       Clarendon.

Blom-Cooper, Louis (Ed.)
1974   Progress in Penal Reform. Oxford: Clarendon.

Bottoms A. E. and F. H. McClintlock
1973   Criminals Coming of Age. London: Heinemann.

Braverman, Harry
1974   Labor and Monopoly Capital: The Degradation of
       Work in the Twentieth Century. New York: Monthly Re-
       view Press.

Burkhart, K. W.
1979   "The concrete womb: 'Getting in'". Pp. 354-371 in F.
       Adler and R.J. Simon (eds.) The Criminology of Deviant
       Women. Boston: Houghton Mifflin.

Canadian Committee on Corrections
1969   Towards Unity: Criminal Justice and Corrections.
       Ottawa: Supply and Services.

Caron, Roger
1979   Go-Boy! (Toronto: Hamlyn).

Carter, Robert M., Daniel Glaser, Leslie T. Wilkins
1972   Correctional Institutions. New York: J. P. Lippin-
       cott.

Clemmer, Donald
1940   The Prison Community. Boston: Christopher

147

Clemmer, Donald
1971 "The process of prisonization". Pp. 92-97 in
L. Radzinowicz and M. Wolfgang (Eds.) The Criminal in
Treatment. New York: Basic Books.

Clinard, Marshall B.
1968 Sociology of Deviant Behaviour. New York: Holt,
Rinehart and Winston.

Cline, H. F.
1968 "The determinants of normative patterns of
correctional institutions". Pp. 173-184 in Christie
(Ed.), Scandinavian Studies in Criminology. London:
Tavistock.

Cloward, Richard and Lloyd Ohlin
1961 Delinquency and Opportunity. New York: Free Press.

Cohen, Albert K.
1955 Delinquent Boys. New York: Free Press.

Cohen, S.
1971 Images of Deviance. Middlesex: Penguin.

Colvin, Mark
1981 "The contradiction of control: Prison in class
society", The Insurgent Sociologist, X, 4; XI, 1 (Sum-
mer-Fall).

Commission of Inquiry into Certain Disturbances at Kingston
Penitentiary During April, 1971.
1971 Report. Ottawa: Supply and Services.

Commission of Inquiry into the Remission Service
1956 Report of the Committee Appointed to Inquire into the
Principles and Procedures followed in the Remission
Service of the Department of Justice of Canada. (Ottawa:
Queen's Printer). (Fauteaux Committee)

Commission of Penitentiaries
1949-1963 Annual Reports. Ottawa.

Conrad, John P.
1974 "Winners and losers: A perspective on penal
change", in Blom-Cooper (Ed.) Progress in Penal
Reform. Oxford: Clarendon.

Coons, W. H.
1982 "Learning disabilities and criminality, Canadian
Journal of Criminology, XXIV, 3 (July): 251-265.

148

Cousineau, F. D. and D. Plecas
    1982 "Justifying criminal justice policy with methodo-
          logically inadequate research", Canadian Journal of
          Criminology, Vol. XXIV, No. 3 (July): 307-321.

Cousineau, F. D. and J. E. Veevers
    1972 "Incarceration as a response to crime: The utilization
          of Canadian prisons." Pp. 135-153 in C. Boydall, C.
          Grindstaff and P. Whitehead (eds.) Deviant Behaviour
          and Societal Reaction. Toronto: Holt, Rinehart and
          Winston.

Cressy, Donald R.
    1972 "Sources of resistance to innovation in corrections".
          Pp. 438-460 in Carter et al. (Eds.) Correctional
          Institutions. New York: J. P. Lippincott.

Cross, Sir Rupert
    1971 Prisons, Punishment and the Public. London: Stevens
          and Sons.

Culhane, Clair
    1981 Chasse de Prison. Montreal: Albert Saint-Martin.

Daires, Louis
    1903 Address delivered to the 6th Canadian Conference
          on Charities and Corrections, Ottawa, Ontario, 29
          Sept.-1 Oct. 1903. Quoted in Department of Labour,
          Labour Gazette, Vol. 4.

Davies, Martin
    1974 Prisoners of Society: Attitudes and After Care.
          London: Routledge and Kegan Paul.

Department of Solicitor General
    1973 The Criminal in Canadian Society: A Perspective on
          Corrections. Ottawa.

Department of Solicitor General
    1976 Annual Report. Ottawa.

Department of Solicitor General
    1976 The Role of Federal Corrections. A Report of the
          Task Force on the Creation of an Integrated Service.
          Ottawa.

Desroches, F. J.
    1981 "The treatment of hostages in prison riots: Some
          hypothesis", Canadian Journal of Criminology,
          Vol. XXIII, No. 4 (October): 439-450.

Desroches, Frederick J.
    1983 "Anomie: Two theories of prison riots", Canadian
          Journal of Criminology, XXV, 2 (April): 173-190.

Douglas, C., J. Drummond and C. Jayewardene
    1980 "Administrative contribution to prison disturbances",
          Canadian Journal of Criminology, XXIII, 4 (October):
          421-438.

Downes, David and Paul Rock
    1979 Deviant Interpretations: Problems in Criminological
          Theory. Oxford: Martin Robertson.

Duguid, Stephen
    1981 "Prison education and criminal choice: The context
          of decision-making", Canadian Journal of Criminology
          Vol. XXIII, No. 4 (October): 421-438.

Durkheim, E.
    1958 Rules of Sociological Method. Glencoe: Free Press.

Ellis, Desmond
    1979 "The prison guard as carceral luddite", Canadian
          Journal of Sociology, IV, 1 (Winter): 43-64.

Ellis, T.
    1974 Quoted in Time, 9 December 1974.

Else, J. and K. Stephenson
    1974 "Vicarious expiation: A theory of prison and social
          reform", Crime and Delinquency, Vol. XX: 359-372.

Emery, F. E.
    1970 Freedom and Justice Within Walls. London.

England, R. W.
    1955 "A study of post-probation recidivism among five
          hundred federal offenders", Federal Probation, Vol.
          19: 10-16.

Enright, Michael
    1977 "The halls of anger", MacLeans, 21 March.

Ericson, Richard
    1975 Criminal Reactions: The Labelling Perspective.
          London: Saxon House.

Ericson, Richard
    1977 "From social theory to penal practice: The liberal
          demise of criminological causes", Canadian Journal of
          Criminology and Corrections, XIX, 2 (April):170-191.

150

Evans, Peter
1980 The Prison Crisis. London: Allen and Unwin.

Farris, Robert E. L.
1955 Social Disorganization. New York: Ronald Press.

Fattah, Ezzat A.
1983 "A critique of deterrence research with particular
       reference to the economic approach", Canadian Journal
       of Criminology, XXV, 1 (January):79-90.

Fitzgerald, Mike
1977 Prisons in Revolt. Harmondsworth: Prnguin.

Fitzgerald, M. and J. Sim
1979 British Prisons. Oxford: Basil Blackwell.

Fontanaro, J. V.
1965 "Canadian prisons today", in W. McGrath (ed.) Crime
       and its Treatment in Canada. Toronto: Macmillan.

Foucault, Michael
1977 Discipline and Punish: The Birth of the Prison.
       New York: Pantheon.

Fox, Vernon
1956 Violence Behind Bars: An Explosive Report on Prison
       Riots in the United States. Westport, Conn.: Green-
       wood.

Friedenberg, Edgar Z.
1980 "The punishment industry in Canada", Canadian
       Journal of Sociology, V, 3 (Summer):273-283.

Garabedian, P. G.
1963 "Social roles and processes of socialization in
       the prison community", Social Problems, Vol. XI: 139-
       152.

Gibbons, D. C.
1960 "Comments on the efficacy of criminal treatment",
       Canadian Journal of Corrections, Vol. II.

Gibbons, D. C.
1977 Society, Crime, and Criminal Careers, (2nd ed.).
       Englewood Cliffs: Prentice Hall.

Gibbons, Don C. and Peter Garabedian
1974 "Conservative, liberal and radical criminology: Some
       trends and observations". Pp. 51-65 in Reasons (Ed.)
       The Criminologist: Crime and the Criminal. Pacific
       Palisades, Calif.: Goodyear.

Gibbons, T. C. N.
1963 Psychiatric Studies of Borstal Lads. London: Oxford University Press.
Giffin, P. J.
1966 "The revolving door: A functional interpretation", Canadian Review of Sociology and Anthropology, III: 154-166.

Gill, Howard B.
1962 "Correctional philosophy and architecture". Journal of Criminal Law, Criminology and Police Science, Vol. LXIII, No. 3: 312-322.

Glaser, Daniel
1964 The Effectiveness of a Prison and Parole System. Indianapolis: Bobbs-Merrill.

Glaser, Daniel
1972 "Disciplinary action and counselling", in Carter et al., Correctional Institutions, New York: Lippincott.

Goffman, E.
1961 Asylums. Garden City, N.J.: Anchor Books.

Gordon, David M.
1974 "Capitalism, class and crime in America". Pp. 66-88 in Reasons (Ed.) The Criminologist: Crime and the Criminal. Pacific Palisades, Calif.: Goodyear.

Gosselin, Luc
1982 Prisons in Canada. Montreal: Black Rose Books.

Gouldner, A.
1968 "The sociologist as partisan: Sociology and the welfare state", American Sociologist, III: 103-116.

Grant,J. D.
1960 "The treatment of non-conformists in the Navy", Annals of the American Academy of Political Science, (March).

Greenberg, David F.
1976 "The incapacitative effects of imprisonment: Some estimates", Law and Society Review, IX.

Grygier, Tadeusz
1965 "The concept of social progression". Pp. 153-193 in Grygier, Jones and Spencer (Eds.) Criminology in Transition: Essays in Honour of Herman Mannheim. London: Tavistock.

Hackler, Jim and Laurel Gould
    1981 "Parole and the violent offender", Canadian Journal
          of Criminology, Vol. XXIII, No. 4 (October): 413-420.

Haley, Hugh J. and Peter Lerette
    1983 Correctional Objectives: The First Step to Accountab-
          ility. (Halifax: Atlantic Institute of Criminology).

Hartung, Frank E. and Maurice Floch
    1956 "A socio-psychological analysis of prison riots: An
          hypothesis", Journal of Criminal Law, Criminology and
          Police Science, XLVII.

Hartzen, Clayton A.
    1974 Crime and Criminalization. New York: Praeger.

Hawkins, Gordon
    1974 "The ideology of imprisonment". In Blom-Cooper (Ed.)
          Progress in Penal Reform. Oxford: Clarendon.

Hofstadter, Richard
    1955 Social Darwinism in American Thought. Boston: Beacon
          Press.

Hogarth, John
    1967 "Toward the improvement of sentencing in Canada",
          Canadian Journal of Corrections, IX: 122-136.

Homer, J.
    1981 "Total institutions and the self-mortification
          process", Canadian Journal of Criminology, XXIII, 3,
          (July):331-342.

Hood, R. G.
    1971 "Some research results and problems". Pp. 159-182
          in L. Radzinowicz and M. Wolfgang (eds.) Crime
          and Justice. New York: Basic Books.

Hood, Roger and Richard Sparks
    1970 Key Issues in Criminology. London: Weidenfeld and
          Nicolson.

Ignatieff, Michael
    1978 A Just Measure of Pain: The Penitentiary in the
          Industrial Revolution 1750-1850. London: Macmillan.

Ignatieff, Michael
    1981 "State, civil society, and total institutions: A
          critique of recent social histories of punishment".
          Pp: 153-192 in M. Tonry and N. Morris (eds.) Crime and
          Justice: An Annual Review of Research. Chicago:
          University of Chicago Press.

153

Irwin, J. and D. R. Cressey
    1962 "Thieves, convicts and the inmate culture", Social
         Problems, Vol. X: 145-155.

Jackson, Margaret A.
    1981 "Review" of Effective Correctional Treatment, by Ross
         and Gendreau, Canadian Journal of Criminology, XXIII,
         4 (October): 473-475.

Jobson, Keith B.
    1977 "Dismantling the system", Canadian Journal of
         Criminology and Corrections, Vol. XIX, No. 3 (July):
         254-272.

Jones, Howard
    1965 "Punishment and social values". Pp. 3-22 in Grygier,
         Jones and Spencer (Eds.) Criminology in Transition.
         London: Tavistock.

Johnston, N.
    1973 The Human Cage: A Brief History of Prison Architec-
         ture. New York: Walker.

Kerr, Madeline
    1958 The People of Ship Street. London: Routledge and
         Kegan Paul.

Kidman, John
    1947 The Canadian Prison: The Story of a Trajedy.
         Toronto: Ryerson Press.

King, Roy D. and Rod Morgan, with J. Martin and J. Thomas
    1980 The Future of the Prison System. Hants, England:
         Gower.

Kirkpatrick, A. M.
    1965 "Penal Reform and Corrections", in Crime and its
         Treatment in Canada, W. T. McGrath (ed.) Toronto:
         Macmillan.

Kirkpatrick, A. M. and W. T. McGrath
    1976 Crime and You. Toronto: McClelland and Stewart.

Lemert, E.
    1967 Human Deviance, Social Problems, and Social Control.
         Englewood Cliffs, N.J.: Prentice Hall.

Lipton, D., R. M. Martinson and J. Wilkes
    1975 The Effectiveness of Correctional Treatment. New
         York: Praeger.

154

MacNaughton-Smith, P.
    1966 Some Statistical and Other Numerical Methods for
          Classifying Individuals. London: HerMajesty's
          Stationery Office, Home Office Research Unit Report
          No. 6.

Mannheim, Hermann and John C. Spencer
    1949 Problems of Classification in the English Penal and
          Reformatory System. London: Institute for the Scienti-
          fic Treatment of Delinquency.

Mannheim, Hermann and Leslie T. Wilkins
    1955 Prediction Methods in Relation to Borstal Training.
          London: Her Majesty's Stationery Office.

Martinson, Robert
    1972 "Planning for public safety", The New Republic,
          Vol. XXIX (April).

Martinson, Robert
    1972 "The Meaning of Attica", The New Republic, 15 April:
          17-19.

Martinson, Robert
    1979 "Restraint and incapacitation: An analytical
          introduction", in M. E. Wolfgang (ed.) Prisons Present
          and Possible. New York: Lexington.

Martzen, Clayton A.
    1974 Crime and Criminalization. New York: Praeger.

Matheson, T.
    1974 The Politics of Abolition. London: Martin Robinson.

McArthur, A. Verne
    1974 Coming Out Cold: Community Re-entry from State
          Reformatory. London: Lexington Books.

McCleary, Richard
    1968 "Correctional administration and political change",
          in L. Hazlenigg (ed.) Prisons Within Society. Garden
          City, N. J.: Doubelday.

McDonald, Lynn
    1976 The Sociology of Law and Order. London: Faber and
          Faber.

McGee, Richard A.
    1972 "Preface", pp. ix-xviii, to Carter et al. (Eds.)
          Correctional Institutions. New York: J. P. Lippincott.

Merton, Robert K.
    1938 "Social structure and anomie", American Sociological
          Review, October.

Morris, Norwal
    1972 "Impediments to Penal Reform". Pp. 461-487 in Carter
          et al., Correctional Institutions. New York: J. P.
          Lippincott.
Morris, T. P.
    1964 "The sociology of the prison". Pp. 69-87 in Grygier
          et al. (Eds.) Criminology in Transition. London:
          Tavistock.

Murphy, B.
    1970 "A quantitative test of the effectiveness of an
          experimental treatment programme for delinquent drug
          users", Unpublished Manuscript, Canadian Penitentiary
          Service.

Murphy, D.
    1984 "Evaluation of a C.C.C." (Paper presented at the
          19th Annual Meetings of the Atlantic Associatiuon of
          Sociologists and Anthropologists, Fredericton, New
          Brunswick, 17 March 1984.

Murton, Thomas O.
    1976 The Dilemma of Prison Reform. New York: Holt, Rine-
          hart and Winston.

Native Counselling Services of Alberta
    1982 "Creating a monster: issues in community program
          control", Canadian Journal of Criminology, XXIV, 3
          (July): 323-328.

Neier, Aryeh
    1976 Crime and Punishment: A Radical Solution. New York:
          Stein and Day.

Opton, E. M.
    1974 "Psychiatric violence against prisoners: When
          therapy is punishment", Mississippi Law Journal, XLV.

Osborne, Thomas Mott
    1916 Society and Prisons: Some Suggestions for a New
          Penology. New Haven: Yale University Press.

Outerbridge, W.
    1968 "The tyranny of treatment", Canadian Journal of
          Corrections, Vol. X.

Pallas, J. and R. Barber
    1976 "From riot to revolution". Pp. 237-261 in E. Wright,
          The Politics of Punishment. New York: Harper and Row.

156

Palmer, Bryan
1980 "Kingston mechanics and the rise of the penitentiary, 1833-1836", Histoire Sociale/Social
History Vol. XIII (May): 7-32.

Parizeau, Alice and Denis Szabo
1977 The Canadian Criminal Justice System. Toronto:
Lexington.

Parliamentary Sub-Committee on the Penitentiary System
1977 Report to Parliament. Ottawa: Supply and Services.

Park, James W. L.
1972 "What is a political prisoner? The politics of
predators", American Journal of Corrections, XXXIV (No-
vember-December).

Phillips, and Votey,
1972 "An ecnomic analysis of the deterrant effects of law
enforcement on criminal activity", Journal of Criminal
Law and Political Science, 63.

Pirzig, Robert
1974 Zen and the Art of Motorcycle Maintenance: An Inquiry
Into Values. New York: Morrow.

Porporino, Frank and Robnert Cormier
1982 "Consensus in decision-making among prison case
management officers", Canadian Journal of Criminology,
XXIV, 3 (July): 279-293.

Powelson, H. and R. Bendix
1951 "Psychiatry in prisons", Psychiatry, XIV.

Pugh, Ralph B.
1968 Imprisonment in Medieval England. Cambridge:
Cambridge University Press.

Quinney, Richard
1970 The Social Reality of Crime. Boston: Little, Brown.

Quinney, Richard
1972 "The ideology of law: Notes for a radical alternative
to legal repression", Issues in Criminology, VII (Win-
ter).

Quinney, Richard
1973 Critique of Legal Order: Crime Control in Capitalist
Society. Boston: Little Brown.

Quinney, Richard
1975 Criminology: Analysis and Critique of Crime in
America. Boston: Little Brown.

Radzinowicz, Leon
  1964 "The criminal in society", Journal of the Royal
        Society of the Arts, 112: 916-929.

Radzinowicz, Leon and Marvin E. Wolfgang (Eds.)
  1971 Crime and Justice. Vol. III, The Criminal in
        Treatment. New York: Basic Books.

Ratner, Robert
  1984 "Inside the liberal boot: Criminological enterprises
        in Canada", Studies in Political Economy, No. 13
        (Spring): 145-164.

Reasons,Charles E.
  1974 "The 'dope' on the Bureau of Narcotics in main-
        taining the criminal approach to the drug problem". In
        Reasons (Ed.) The Criminologist: Crime and the Crim-
        inal. Pacific Palisades, Calif.: Goodyear.

Reasons, Charles E. (Ed.)
  1974 The Criminologist: Crime and the Criminal.
        Pacific Palisades, Calif.: Goodyear.

Reasons, Charles E.
  1975 "Social thought and social structure: Competing
        paradigms in criminology", Criminology, Vol. XIII: 332-
        365.

Reasons, Charles E.
  1977 "On methodology, theory and ideology", American
        Sociological Review, 42: 177-188.

Reker, Gary T. and John A. Meissner
  1977 "Life skills in Canadian federal penitentiaries: An
        experimental evaluation", Canadian Journal of Crimino-
        logy and Corrections, XIX, 3 (July): 292-302.

Richmond, Mark S. and George W. Aderhold
  1972 "New roles for jails", in Carter et al. Correctional
        Institutions. New York: J. P. Lippincott.

Ross, V.
  1983 "Inside Canada's Prisons", Macleans, 6 June 1983:
        16-22.

Rothman, David J.
  1971 The Discovery of the Asylum: Social Order and Disorder
        in the New Republic. Boston: Little, Brown.

Rothman, David J.
  1980 Conscience and Convenience: The Asylum and its Alterna-
        tives in Progressive America. Toronto: Little, Brown.

158

Schrag, Clarence
1971 "Leadership among prison inmates". Pp. 85-90 in
L. Radzinowicz and M. Wolfgang, Criminal in Treatment.
New York: Basic Books.

Schroeder, Andreas
1967 Shaking it Rough: A Prison Memoir. Toronto:
Doubleday.

Schur, E.
1971 Labelling Deviant Behaviour: Its Sociological
Implications. New York: Harper and Row.

Schwendinger, H. and J. Schwendinger
1975 "Defenders of order or guardians of human rights?" In
I. Taylor et al. (eds.) Critical Criminology. Boston:
Routledge and Kegan Paul.

Sellin, Thorstein
1972 "Corrections in historical perspective". Pp. 8-16 in
Carter et al. (Eds.) Correctional Institutions. New
York: J. P. Lippincott.

Spencer, J. C.
n.d. "Problems in Transition: From Prison to Therapeutic
Community". Mimeo.

Spinley, Betty
1953 The Deprived and the Privileged. London: Routledge
and Kegan Paul.

Stang, David P.
1974 "Problems of the corrections system". In C. Reasons
(ed.) The Criminologist.

Statistics Canada
1975 Penitentiary Statistics. Ottawa: Supply and Services.

Sullivan, Dennis
1980 The Mask of Love: Corrections in America. New York:
National University Publications.

Superintendent of Penitentiaries
1937 Annual Report. Ottawa.

Sutherland, E. H.
1949 White Collar Crime. New York: Dryden.

Sutherland, Edwin H. and Donald R. Cressey
1970 Criminology. 8th Ed. Philadelphia: J. P. Lippincott.

Sykes, Gresham
　　1958　The Society of Captives. Princeton, N. J.: University Press.

Sykes, Gresham and Sheldon Messinger
　　1971　"Inmate social system". Pp. 77-85 in Radzinowicz and Wolfgang (Eds.) The Criminal in Treatment. New York: Basic Books.

Tannenbaum, Frank
　　1938　Crime and Community. Boston: Ginn.

Tappan, Paul W.
　　1960　Crime, Justice and Correction. New York: McGraw-Hill.

Task Force on Community-Based Residential Centres
　　1972　Report. Ottawa Supply and Services.

Taylor, Ian
　　1984　"Social policy and future criminal justice developments in Canada: A Socialist perspective", (Paper presented for the Atlantic Institute of Criminology Distinguished Speakers Series, Halifax, Nova Scotia, 1 May 1984.)

Taylor, Ian, Paul Walton and Jock Young
　　1973　The New Criminology. London: Routledge and Kegan Paul.

Tepperman, Lorne
　　1977　Crime Control: The Urge Towards Authority. Toronto: McGraw-Hill Ryerson.

Thio, Alex
　　1975　"Class bias in the sociology of deviance". Pp. 272-291 in Stuart H. Traub and Craig B. Little, Theories of Deviance. Uasca, Ill.: Peacock.

Tittle, C. S.
　　1972　"Institutional living and self-esteem", Social Problems, XX: 65-77.

Topping, C. W.
　　1930　Canadian Penal Institutions. Chicago: University of Chicago Press.

Trasler, G.
　　1972　"The role of psychologists in the penal system", Pp. 129-141 in L. Blom-Cooper (ed.) Progress in Penal Reform. Oxford: Clarendon.

160

Trepanier, Jean
1981 "La dejudiciarisation des mineurs delinquants au
Canada", Canadian Journal of Criminology, XXIII, 3
(July): 279-289.

Turk, Austin T.
1969 Criminality and Legal Order. Chicago: Rand McNally.

Vogelman, Richard P.
1968 "Prison restrictions--prison rights", Journal of
Criminal Law, Criminology and Police Science, Vol. LIX,
No. 3: 386-396.

Vold, George B.
1954 "Does the prison reform?" Annals of the American
Academy of Political and Social Science, 293, May:
173-184.

Vold, George B.
1958 Theoretical Criminology. New York: Oxford University
Press.

Walker, Peter N.
1972 Punishment: An Illustrated History. Newton Abbot,
Devonshire: David and Charles.

Waller, I.
1971 Men Released from Prison: A Means Towards Understanding
the Correctional Effectiveness of Parole. Toronto:
Centre of Criminology.

Warren, M.
1977 "Correctional treatment and coercion", Criminal
Justice and Behavior, Vol. iv.

Wheeler, Stanton
1971 "Socialization in correctional institutions". Pp.
97-116 in L. Radzinowicz and M. Wolfgang (Eds.) The
Criminal in Treatment. New York: Basic Books.

Wheeler, Stanton and Leonard S. Cottrell
1969 "The labeling process". Pp. 608-612 in Cressey and
Ward (eds). Delinquency, Crime, and Social Process.
New York: Harper and Row.

Wilkins, L. T.
1958 "A small comparative study of the results of
probation", British Journal of Delinquency, Vol. 8:
201-209.

Wilkins, L. T.
1969 Evaluations of Penal Measures. New York: Random
House.

Wills, Garry
    1975   "The Human Sewer", New York Review, 3 April.

Wolfgang, M. E.
    1960   "Cesare Lombroso", in Hermann Mannheim (Ed.) Pio-
            neers in Criminology. London: Stevens.

Wright, Eric Olin
    1973   The Politics of Punishment: A Critical Analysis of
            Prisons in America. New York: Harper and Row.

Wright, Kevin N. (Ed.)
    1981   Crime and Criminal Justice in a Declining Economy.
            Cambridge, Mass.

Zeitlin, Irving M.
    1981   Ideology and the Development of Sociological
            Theory. Toronto: Prentics-Hall.